ANOINTED

To Suffer · To Serve · To Save

A Flexible Inductive Study of

ISAIAH 53

BY

PAM GILLASPIE

Anointed: To Suffer • To Serve • To Save

Dedicated to . . .

God's people—first to the natural branches and then to the wild ones grafted in.

Acknowledgements

My most sincere thanks to my fellow students at New Hope Christian Community Church and at Immanuel Church who piloted this material with me. I am grateful to walk with you and learn together. Thanks, too, to Rick Purdy and Pete DeLacy for your theological and editorial input and guidance. Finally, thanks to my dear husband for the cover design and for your constant encouragement to follow God's call on my life. Your support means the world to me!

ANOINTED
TO SUFFER · TO SERVE · TO SAVE

ANOINTED

To Suffer · To Serve · To Save

There is nothing quite like your favorite pair of jeans. You can dress them up, you can dress them down. You can work in them, play in them, shop in them . . . live in them. They always feel right. It is my hope that the structure of this Bible study will fit you like those jeans; that it will work with your life right now, right where you are whether you're new to this whole Bible thing or whether you've been studying the Book for years!

How is this even possible? Smoke and mirrors, perhaps? The new mercilessly thrown in the deep end? The experienced given pompoms and the job of simply cheering others on? None of the above.

Sweeter than Chocolate!® flexible studies are designed with options that will allow you to go as deep each week as you desire. If you're just starting out and feeling a little overwhelmed, stick with the main text and don't think a second thought about the sidebar assignments. If you're looking for a challenge, then take the sidebar prompts and go ahead and dig all the way to China! As you move along through the study, think of the sidebars and "Digging Deeper" boxes as that 2% of lycra that you find in certain jeans . . . the wiggle-room that will help them fit just right.

Beginners may find that they want to start adding in some of the optional assignments as they go along. Experts may find that when three children are throwing up for three days straight, foregoing those assignments for the week is the way to live wisely.

Life has a way of ebbing and flowing and this study is designed to ebb and flow right along with it!

Enjoy!

CONTENTS

ANOINTED
To Suffer · To Serve · To Save

How to use this study

Sweeter than Chocolate!® studies meet you where you are and take you as far as you want to go.

1. **WEEKLY STUDY:** The main text guides you through the complete topic of study for the week.

2. **FYI boxes:** For Your Information boxes provide bite-sized material to shed additional light on the topic.

3. **ONE STEP FURTHER and other sidebar boxes:** Sidebar boxes give you the option to push yourself a little further. If you have extra time or are looking for an extra challenge, you can try one, all, or any number in between! These boxes give you the ultimate in flexibility.

4. **DIGGING DEEPER boxes:** If you're looking to go further, Digging Deeper sections will help you sharpen your skills as you continue to mine the truths of Scripture for yourself.

ANOINTED
TO SUFFER · TO SERVE · TO SAVE

LESSON ONE
The Mysterious Servant

"Behold, My servant will prosper,
He will be high and lifted up and greatly exalted."
–Isaiah 52:13

Life's burdens weigh down even the strongest. Whether you're weakened by sorrow and grief, laid low by suffering and hardship, or failing under the weight of your own sin, you know the weight of life. You know it. I know it. Everyone knows it. Deeds done that cannot be undone. Words spoken that can never be called back. Wrongs committed in fleeting moments that sear consciences for a lifetime.

The 53rd chapter of Isaiah, a writing common to both the Jewish Tanakh and the Christian Bible, describes a mysterious figure who provides the solution for the human condition by carrying griefs and sorrows, healing brokenness, and bearing sin. He is the Servant of the Lord!

But who is this person? Who is this Servant of the Lord? In this study, we'll look closely at Isaiah 53 to answer this question for ourselves. As we start off, though, let's put ourselves in context by examining the final words of Isaiah 52.

FYI:

If You're in a Class
Begin **Week One** together on your first day of class. This will be a great way to start getting to know one another and will help those who are newer to Bible study get their bearings.

ANOINTED
TO SUFFER · TO SERVE · TO SAVE

CONSIDER the WAY YOU THINK

We all come to Bible study with different views and experiences. Before we get started, let's consider some of those together.

What is your view of the Bible? Do you think it is a work of man? A work of God? A little of both? Or are you not quite sure? Why?

Do you think your view of the Bible impacts how you respond to what you read? Explain.

Are you familiar with the prophet Isaiah? What about Isaiah 53 specifically? If so, what do you know about it? (If not, don't worry. You'll be familiar with it soon!)

FYI:

Letting the Text Speak

As we study together, it is my prayer that to the best of our ability we will drop our presuppositions and allow God's Word to speak for itself. There so much freedom in this, isn't there? You don't have to come up with clever ideas and remotely possible "what if?"s. You simply pay attention and learn from what God has clearly revealed.

When we do this it's called *exegesis*. Exegesis literally means "to lead out." When we deal in presuppositions and subjectivism we're falling into the trap of eisegesis (literally "to lead into")–taking the text of Scripture and tailoring it to our agendas. Eisegesis molds Scripture to fit man; the Word accurately handled calls man to submit to the plumb line of Scripture. My goal in this class is to handle accurately the Word of truth and have God speak to us and change *us* through it.

GETTING THE BIG PICTURE

This week we'll be looking at the Servant Song in Isaiah 52:13–53:12 for a general overview. So, if you start feeling confused or overwhelmed at any point, just take a second and breathe. The first part of inductive Bible study–observation–is all about slowing down, reading the text carefully and asking questions. We wouldn't need to ask questions if we already knew the answers, right?

In upcoming weeks, we'll look much more closely at the text to determine if and how the prophecy was eventually fulfilled. Right now, though, as we overview the text, we will focus on some of the unique features of the servant described in Isaiah 53 and the verses leading up to it. We'll want to keep a couple of questions in the front of our mind as we read: Who **could** this be referring to? and Who could this **not** be referring to?

ANOINTED
To Suffer · To Serve · To Save

OBSERVE the TEXT of SCRIPTURE

READ Isaiah 52:13–53:12 and **MARK** every reference to the *servant* including pronouns. You'll be marking mostly pronouns (*He, Him, His* with reference to the *servant*).

Isaiah 52:13-15

13   Behold, My servant will prosper,
      He will be high and lifted up and greatly exalted.

14   Just as many were astonished at you, My people,
      So His appearance was marred more than any man
      And His form more than the sons of men.

15   Thus He will sprinkle many nations,
      Kings will shut their mouths on account of Him;
      For what had not been told them they will see,
      And what they had not heard they will understand.

Isaiah 53

1   Who has believed our message?
     And to whom has the arm of the LORD been revealed?

2   For He grew up before Him like a tender shoot,
     And like a root out of parched ground;
     He has no stately form or majesty
     That we should look upon Him,
     Nor appearance that we should be attracted to Him.

3   He was despised and forsaken of men,
     A man of sorrows and acquainted with grief;
     And like one from whom men hide their face
     He was despised, and we did not esteem Him.

4   Surely our griefs He Himself bore,
     And our sorrows He carried;
     Yet we ourselves esteemed Him stricken,
     Smitten of God, and afflicted.

5   But He was pierced through for our transgressions,
     He was crushed for our iniquities;
     The chastening for our well-being fell upon Him,
     And by His scourging we are healed.

6   All of us like sheep have gone astray,
     Each of us has turned to his own way;
     But the LORD has caused the iniquity of us all
     To fall on Him.

7   He was oppressed and He was afflicted,
     Yet He did not open His mouth;
     Like a lamb that is led to slaughter,
     And like a sheep that is silent before its shearers,
     So He did not open His mouth.

8   By oppression and judgment He was taken away;
     And as for His generation, who considered
     That He was cut off out of the land of the living
     For the transgression of my people, to whom the stroke was due?

FYI:

Start with Prayer

You've probably heard it before and if we study together in the future, you're sure to hear it again. Whenever you read or study God's Word, first pray and ask His Spirit to be your Guide. Jesus says that the Spirit will lead us into all truth.

INDUCTIVE STUDY:

What is Inductive study?

When we study the Bible inductively, we simply use the Bible as our primary source in studying the Bible. While it sounds beyond obvious, much of what people term "Bible study" today is more of a compilation of others' opinions about the Bible, rather than biblical truth direct from the source.

In inductive study, we seek to allow God to speak for Himself as we discover truth directly from His Word.

ANOINTED
TO SUFFER · TO SERVE · TO SAVE

9 *His grave was assigned with wicked men,*
   Yet He was with a rich man in His death,
   Because He had done no violence,
   Nor was there any deceit in His mouth.

10 *But the LORD was pleased*
   To crush Him, putting Him to grief;
   If He would render Himself as a guilt offering,
   He will see His offspring,
   He will prolong His days,
   And the good pleasure of the LORD will prosper in His hand.

11 *As a result of the anguish of His soul,*
   He will see it and be satisfied;
   By His knowledge the Righteous One,
   My Servant, will justify the many,
   As He will bear their iniquities.

12 *Therefore, I will allot Him a portion with the great,*
   And He will divide the booty with the strong;
   Because He poured out Himself to death,
   And was numbered with the transgressors;
   Yet He Himself bore the sin of many,
   And interceded for the transgressors.

DISCUSS with your GROUP or PONDER on your own . . .
WHO, WHAT, WHEN, WHERE, WHY, and HOW

Who recorded these words in Scripture? (If you're not sure, don't stress. Move on to the next question.)

Approximately when was this written? If you're not sure, read Isaiah 1:1.

Who was this written to? Where did the initial recipients live?

FYI:

The Backstory of Isaiah's Audience

The Bible's opening book of Genesis lays the foundation for all of the accounts that follow. In it we learn that God created everything that has ever existed including mankind. When Adam and Eve, the first created people, rebelled against God sin and death entered the world, but it did not catch God off guard. He already had a rescue plan in place that would come through Adam's line.

Adam and Eve had children who had children. Some of the more notable names in the Genesis account include Noah (who God delivered along with his family from a worldwide flood), Abraham, Isaac, and Jacob. Jacob was the father of the nation of Israel that Egypt enslaved for 400 years.

God delivered the Israelites from Egypt by the hand of Moses and eventually used Joshua to lead them into the Promised Land (what we know today as the land of Israel). After Joshua died, Judges ruled the land until the people called for a king.

Isaiah wrote toward the end of the time of the kings. Israel, the united kingdom of 12 tribes, had already dissolved.

The one country has become two. In the Northern Kingdom which retained the name "Israel," non-Davidic kings rule over 10 tribes. In the Southern Kingdom of Judah, descendants of King David lead the remaining 2 tribes.

Isaiah's ministry is primarily to these southern tribes.

ANOINTED
TO SUFFER · TO SERVE · TO SAVE

Who is the subject of Isaiah 52:13–53:12? Is He specifically identified? Explain.

What basic information do we learn about Him? (This is where you'll want to look at every place you've marked either *servant* or a pronoun—*He, His, Himself*—referring to the servant and make a simple list.)

Which of these facts did you find most interesting or significant? Why?

Although Isaiah doesn't name the servant, what title does he give Him in verse 11? What is significant about the title?

Why do you think so many consider this an important text?

How do you think we can find out who the servant is . . . and isn't?

FYI:

Historical Information

According to Isaiah 1:1, Isaiah prophesied during the reigns of four kings of Judah: Uzziah (also known as Azariah), Jotham, Ahaz, and Hezekiah. His ministry began in the year that King Uzziah died (c. 739) and he prophesied during the reigns of the subsequent three kings of Judah. During this time, the Northern Kingdom of Israel fell to the Assyrians in 722 BC. Tradition holds that Isaiah died at the hands of Hezekiah's son Manasseh, having been sawn in two (Hebrews 11:37).

Isaiah warned the people of coming judgment during tumultuous and rebellious days, but he also offered comfort and hope of God's ultimate salvation.

FYI:

Isaiah's Call

1 "In the year of King Uzziah's death I saw the Lord sitting on a throne, lofty and exalted, with the train of His robe filling the temple."

8 "Then I heard the voice of the Lord, saying, "Whom shall I send, and who will go for Us?" Then I said, "Here am I. Send me!"

—Isaiah 6:1, 8

ANOINTED
To Suffer · To Serve · To Save

THE GREATER CONTEXT and DIFFERING VIEWS

While the servant described in Isaiah 53 is an innocent sin bearer, the near context of Isaiah also talks about other less than perfect servants. Let's take a brief look at the use of the Hebrew word *ebed* in Isaiah and consider how this might affect interpretation. If you want to look at this further, check out the **One Step Further** option in the margin!

OBSERVE the TEXT of SCRIPTURE

READ the following verses from Isaiah and **MARK** the word *servant* in each. Then record what the verses say about: 1) who the servant is, and 2) who the servant belongs to (if applicable).

Isaiah 14:2

2   The peoples will take them along and bring them to their place, and the house of Israel will possess them as an inheritance in the land of the LORD as male servants and female servants; and they will take their captors captive and will rule over their oppressors.

The servants are . . .

Isaiah 20:3-4

3   And the LORD said, "Even as My servant Isaiah has gone naked and barefoot three years as a sign and token against Egypt and Cush,

4   so the king of Assyria will lead away the captives of Egypt and the exiles of Cush, young and old, naked and barefoot with buttocks uncovered, to the shame of Egypt.

The servant is . . .

Isaiah 22:20-21

20   "Then it will come about in that day, that I will summon My servant Eliakim the son of Hilkiah,

21   And I will clothe him with your tunic and tie your sash securely about him. I will entrust him with your authority, and he will become a father to the inhabitants of Jerusalem and to the house of Judah.

The servant is . . .

Isaiah 37:35

35   'For I will defend this city to save it for My own sake and for My servant David's sake.' "

The servant is . . .

Isaiah 41:8-9

8   "But you, Israel, My servant, Jacob whom I have chosen, descendant of Abraham My friend,

9   You whom I have taken from the ends of the earth, and called from its remotest parts and said to you, 'You are My servant, I have chosen you and not rejected you.

The servant is . . .

Isaiah 42:18-22

18   Hear, you deaf! And look, you blind, that you may see.

19   Who is blind but My servant, or so deaf as My messenger whom I send? Who is so blind as he that is at peace with Me, or so blind as the servant of the LORD?

20   You have seen many things, but you do not observe them; your ears are open, but none hears.

21   The LORD was pleased for His righteousness' sake to make the law great and glorious.

22   But this is a people plundered and despoiled; all of them are trapped in caves, or are hidden away in prisons; they have become a prey with none to deliver them, and a spoil, with none to say, "Give them back!"

The servant is . . .

FYI:

Resources
There are so many tremendous online resources for studying the Bible today! Here are a couple of my favorites:

• blueletterbible.org

• biblehub.com

• thebible.org

If you have some favorites, jot them down below and be sure to share them with your classmates!

•

•

•

•

•

ANOINTED
To Suffer · To Serve · To Save

DISCUSS with your GROUP or PONDER on your own . . .

Summarize the different ways you've observed "servant" used in Isaiah.

ONE STEP FURTHER:

The Tanakh

Before we wrap up our study this week, take the time to read Isaiah 52:13–53:12 once more, but this time from the Tanakh—the Hebrew Bible.

On your internet browser, simply search for "Isaiah 53 JPS." This will take you to the Jewish Publication Society translation of Isaiah 53.

Did you notice any significant differences in the translation? List what you observed and note how it compares with the NASB.

Do you think that any of the "servants" you looked at this week could be the One referred to in Isaiah 53? Why/why not? Explain your answer from Scripture.

Digging Deeper

More of the Story

If you're looking for more this week, take some time to read Isaiah 40–54 to see the greater context of Isaiah 53 and the other Servant Songs first hand! As you read consider the following questions:

What is the main content of Isaiah 40–54?

How does Isaiah 53 fit into this context?

How is the word "servant" (and its pronouns) used in these chapters?

ANOINTED
To Suffer · To Serve · To Save

What else did you observe about this section of Isaiah?

What other questions do you have?

@THE END OF THE DAY . . .

What a promise Isaiah 53 offers—a sin bearer for those weighed down by their own offenses, a healer for the broken and sorrowful. What pains are you carrying today? What griefs can you no longer bear? There is hope in the One the prophets of Israel pointed to. There is hope in the Righteous One!

Lesson Two: **The Mysterious Servant**

LESSON TWO
Who Has Believed? Have You?

"Who has believed our message?
And to whom has the arm of the LORD been revealed?"

–Isaiah 53:1

The people of Israel knew their God as a deliverer! When they were downtrodden by Pharaoh, king of Egypt, when they were oppressed under a people stronger than themselves year after year after year, God Himself intervened to save them. After 400 years of slavery, God brought a world power to its knees and set His people free!

The Israelites experienced God's wonders first-hand as He brought plagues upon Egypt, then commanded His people to remind their children of them. Throughout their generations, the people of Israel watched God deliver them from one enemy after another—in the wilderness wanderings, as they entered and possessed the Promised Land, and during the times of the judges and of kings of Israel. Over and over, time and again, as the people cried out for help, God sent deliverers who won military victories for the nation and saved them from their enemies.

The Deliverer of Isaiah 53, though, is different in kind, unlike anything they'd experienced before or could ever imagine or expect! To many He was simply unbelievable.

FYI:

NASB, ESV, and JPS
The NASB and ESV are reliable word-for-word translations of the original languages of the Old and New Testaments. While the KJV and NKJV are also translated word for word, they do not include consideration of earlier-dated original-language manuscripts discovered more recently.

The JPS is a translation of the Tanakh, the Hebrew Bible, by the Jewish Publication Society.

FYI:

It's a One-Chapter Study!
If you start feeling overwhelmed at any point this week, remember this: *It's a one-chapter study!* If you can't get to the homework that's okay, just go to the text. And did I mention our main text is only ONE CHAPTER? That's right, one chapter and not even a long one. No matter how busy you are this week, you can find or make some time to read 12 verses through once or twice. I'm sure of it!

ANOINTED
To Suffer · To Serve · To Save

REMEMBERING

Take a few minutes to summarize what you learned last week.

WEEKLY OBSERVATION

We'll keep all of Isaiah 53 in front of us each week as we drive deeper into the text verse by verse.

OBSERVE the TEXT of SCRIPTURE

READ Isaiah 53 and **MARK** references to the LORD in a distinctive fashion. Be sure to include any synonyms (e.g. *God*) and pronouns (*He, His, I, My*, etc.) that refer to Him.

Isaiah 53

1 *Who has believed our message?*
   And to whom has the arm of the LORD been revealed?

2 *For He grew up before Him like a tender shoot,*
   And like a root out of parched ground;
   He has no stately form or majesty
   That we should look upon Him,
   Nor appearance that we should be attracted to Him.

3 *He was despised and forsaken of men,*
   A man of sorrows and acquainted with grief;
   And like one from whom men hide their face
   He was despised, and we did not esteem Him.

4 *Surely our griefs He Himself bore,*
   And our sorrows He carried;
   Yet we ourselves esteemed Him stricken,
   Smitten of God, and afflicted.

5 *But He was pierced through for our transgressions,*
   He was crushed for our iniquities;
   The chastening for our well-being fell upon Him,
   And by His scourging we are healed.

6 *All of us like sheep have gone astray,*
   Each of us has turned to his own way;
   But the LORD has caused the iniquity of us all
   To fall on Him.

INDUCTIVE FOCUS:

Help! How do I mark?

As you mark the text, be as creative or as simple as you like. Marking is simply a way to help key words stand out on the page, so do whatever works best for you in that regard.

One strategy that works well for me is keeping similar words or ideas tied with particular colors. For example, I typically mark references to God with purple, since purple is the color of royalty. While I use a purple triangle for God (the triangle to represent the Trinity), I often use a purple circle for Levites who work in the service of God. Prophets often end up with purple, too.

I use brown as my color for sin and sinners while green is the color I associate with life/eternal life. I use a blue underline for righteous/righteousness, and a light blue circle for faith/belief. Why? Not sure, but since faith shows up often in the Word I wanted a simple way to mark it and a color that I liked—next thing you know it was a light blue circle.

While I could go on about this all day, I'll wrap up with this final example. I use pink for any references to female characters—since they are a little more rare, I like to be able to find them quickly—and I underline references to wisdom in pink as Proverbs speaks about wisdom as a woman.

Do what makes sense to you and always remember that colored pencils and pens are tools. You're in charge of them. Make them work for you, not the other way around!

7 He was oppressed and He was afflicted,
    Yet He did not open His mouth;
    Like a lamb that is led to slaughter,
    And like a sheep that is silent before its shearers,
    So He did not open His mouth.

8 By oppression and judgment He was taken away;
    And as for His generation, who considered
    That He was cut off out of the land of the living
    For the transgression of my people, to whom the stroke was due?

9 His grave was assigned with wicked men,
    Yet He was with a rich man in His death,
    Because He had done no violence,
    Nor was there any deceit in His mouth.

10 But the LORD was pleased
    To crush Him, putting Him to grief;
    If He would render Himself as a guilt offering,
    He will see His offspring,
    He will prolong His days,
    And the good pleasure of the LORD will prosper in His hand.

11 As a result of the anguish of His soul,
    He will see it and be satisfied;
    By His knowledge the Righteous One,
    My Servant, will justify the many,
    As He will bear their iniquities.

12 Therefore, I will allot Him a portion with the great,
    And He will divide the booty with the strong;
    Because He poured out Himself to death,
    And was numbered with the transgressors;
    Yet He Himself bore the sin of many,
    And interceded for the transgressors.

DISCUSS with your GROUP or PONDER on your own . . .

Look back at where you marked references to the LORD. What did you learn about Him? What did you learn about Him in relation to the Servant? You may want to make a list.

INDUCTIVE FOCUS:

Questioning the Text

The key to exegesis (the fancy word for discovering what Scripture says) is questioning the text. As we read, we'll address the basic investigative questions *Who? What? When? Where? Why?* and *How?* to the texts.

You'll quickly realize that there's a limit to the number of questions we can ask from week to week in a workbook format. If we ask too many, people will run away screaming—don't laugh, it's happened! That said, don't let the inherent limitations of a class stop you from asking other questions and exploring further on your own! We will never run out of questions to ask and answers to glean from God's Word!

If you're at a loss for what questions to ask, pay attention to the words that you've marked. Go to your key words and start there with your questions! Marking helps you see key words and frame questions. As you answer the questions, you'll begin to see main ideas or themes in the passage unfold.

Remember to pray for the Spirit's guidance in this process and then slow down and pay attention to His revealed Word.

ANOINTED
TO SUFFER · TO SERVE · TO SAVE

LOOKING CLOSER . . .

As we look at the text more closely, we'll proceed verse by verse. Our focus this week will be on just two verses—Isaiah 53:1-2. Breathe. Enjoy. And, maybe, let's memorize! It could be fun!

ONE STEP FURTHER:

The Arm of the LORD

If you have time this week, use Blueletterbible.org to run a concordance search on the word "arm" (Hebrew: *zeroa*) that appears in Isaiah 53:1. By searching on *zeroa*, you'll be able to see everywhere that particular word appears throughout the Old Testament. Pay particular attention to the phrase "arm of the Lord."

Make note of how it is used in Isaiah and the rest of the Old Testament and then record your observations below.

If you're not sure how to do this, you can find step-by-step instructions in the Resources section at the back of the workbook.

OBSERVE the TEXT of SCRIPTURE

READ Isaiah 53:1-2 and **MARK** any words of interest.

Isaiah 53:1-2

1   Who has believed our message?
    And to whom has the arm of the LORD been revealed?

2   For He grew up before Him like a tender shoot,
    And like a root out of parched ground;
    He has no stately *form or majesty*
    That we should look upon Him,
    Nor appearance that we should be attracted to Him.

DISCUSS with your GROUP or PONDER on your own . . .

What two questions does Isaiah 53:1 ask?

Can we identify the speaker(s)? What can we deduce from the text about this? (Base your answer on what you see in the whole chapter and note if you see any shifts from one speaker to another.)

What message has been delivered or reported? (Again, use all of Isaiah 53 to answer.)

What do you think is involved in believing this message?

More of the story . . . the arm of the LORD

In order to understand better what the phrase "the arm of the LORD" means, let's do some cross-reference work. Cross-referencing is a way we can use Scripture to help us interpret Scripture. In this case, we'll look at references to God's arm as He delivers Israel from Egypt.

As we pick up the text in Exodus 6, the sons of Israel are enslaved under the hand of Pharaoh but God sends Moses to them to announce that He will deliver them from the Egyptians. The Deuteronomy text which follows comes 40 years after the deliverance when God tells His people to remember what He has done for them.

Always remember you can go directly to your own Bible for more of the context!

OBSERVE the TEXT of SCRIPTURE

READ Exodus 6:6 and Deuteronomy 5:15 and **MARK** *outstretched arm.*

Exodus 6:6

6 *"Say, therefore, to the sons of Israel, 'I am the LORD, and I will bring you out from under the burdens of the Egyptians, and I will deliver you from their bondage. I will also redeem you with an outstretched arm and with great judgments.'"*

Deuteronomy 5:15

15 *"'You shall remember that you were a slave in the land of Egypt, and the LORD your God brought you out of there by a mighty hand and by an outstretched arm; therefore the LORD your God commanded you to observe the sabbath day.'"*

DISCUSS with your GROUP or PONDER on your own . . .

What does the LORD's arm refer to in each of these verses? What is it associated with?

How did God deliver the people from Egypt? What did the mighty hand and the outstretched arm do to the Egyptians and for the Israelites?

Based on these verses, what might you expect "the arm of the LORD" to refer to in Isaiah 53:1?

ONE STEP FURTHER:

The Exodus

If you've never read about Israel's deliverance from Egypt first hand, you can check it out for yourself in Exodus 1–13. There's room below to record a simple summary.

ANOINTED
To Suffer · To Serve · To Save

15

Digging Deeper

Let's Remember Together . . . Isaiah 53:1-2

The older I get, the more I am convinced that slowing down enough to actually memorize is the best way to do inductive study AND that studying the Bible inductively is the best way to memorize. Because of this and because our main text for this class is only 12 verses long, I'm going to incorporate memorizing Isaiah 53 into our Digging Deeper sections along the way. As I do this, I'm going to break down the text in a way that makes it easier for us to encode and eventually remember.

Isaiah 53:1 opens with TWO QUESTIONS that have to do with an announcement about God's power and coming deliverance.

TWO QUESTIONS:

Who has	**believed**	**our message?** (of God's deliverance)
And to whom has	**the arm of the LORD** (God's deliverance)	**been revealed?**

Having set up the readers to expect the announcement of a powerful deliverer, verse 2 presents UNEXPECTED information.

1. THE DELIVERER IS COMPARED TO A PLANT:

He grew up before (the Deliverer)	**Him** (God)	**like a tender shoot,**
And		**like a root out of a parched ground;**

Instead of shock-and-awe deliverance like the Egyptian plagues and the parting of the Red Sea, the promised Deliverer is described as a young plant growing up in dry earth.

2. THE DELIVERER IS NOTHING SPECIAL TO LOOK AT:

He has no stately form or majesty (the Deliverer)	**That we should look upon Him,**
Nor appearance	**that we should be attracted to Him.**

As you memorize, pay attention to all of the parallel phrases (I've done the best I can to try and emphasize them in the text), to help you with "handholds" to grab onto as you review and recall. You won't have to use these forever, but they will help you to remember the text logically while you're committing it to your long-term, recite-it-backwards-while-standing-on-your-head memory.

ONE STEP FURTHER:

Tender Shoot

If you have time this week, take a look at the Hebrew word translated "tender shoot" in Isaiah 53:2. Using Blueletterbible.org or another resource, find the Hebrew word and record what you discover about it below.

More of the story . . . the tender shoot

The metaphorical tender shoot points to a specific person. Let's take a look at a couple Old Testament passages that shed some light. In 2 Samuel 7 King David wants to build a temple for God, but God sends word through the prophet Nathan that He is going to do something for David instead. In the Isaiah 11 passage, remember that the name of David's father is Jesse. Let's take a look.

OBSERVE the TEXT of SCRIPTURE

READ 2 Samuel 7:11b-13 and **MARK** *descendant*. Be sure to include pronouns.

2 Samuel 7:11b-13

11b The LORD also declares to you that the LORD will make a house for you.

12 "When your days are complete and you lie down with your fathers, I will raise up your descendant after you, who will come forth from you, and I will establish his kingdom.

13 "He shall build a house for My name, and I will establish the throne of his kingdom forever.

OBSERVE the TEXT of SCRIPTURE

READ Isaiah 11:1-10 and **MARK** plant references (*shoot, stem, branch, roots*). Then **MARK** words including pronouns that refer to the "shoot"/"branch" of verse 1. Finally, **MARK** any time phrases you notice.

Isaiah 11:1-10

1 Then a shoot will spring from the stem of Jesse,
And a branch from his roots will bear fruit.

2 The Spirit of the LORD will rest on Him,
The spirit of wisdom and understanding,
The spirit of counsel and strength,
The spirit of knowledge and the fear of the LORD.

3 And He will delight in the fear of the LORD,
And He will not judge by what His eyes see,
Nor make a decision by what His ears hear;

4 But with righteousness He will judge the poor,
And decide with fairness for the afflicted of the earth;
And He will strike the earth with the rod of His mouth,
And with the breath of His lips He will slay the wicked.

5 Also righteousness will be the belt about His loins,
And faithfulness the belt about His waist.

6 And the wolf will dwell with the lamb,
And the leopard will lie down with the young goat,
And the calf and the young lion and the fatling together;
And a little boy will lead them.

ONE STEP FURTHER:

The Rest of the Story

If you're not familiar with God's promise to King David—often referred to as the Davidic Covenant—take some time this week to read about it in 2 Samuel 7. Record what you learn below.

FYI:

Part of the Family Tree

It's amazing: the people that God uses! Here's a partial list of the folks in David's family tree going back to his great, great grandparents. Even when He was working primarily with Israel, God's missionary heart in saving Rahab and Ruth is evident.

Great, Great Grandparents:

Rahab the Canaanite Harlot and Salmon the Israelite

Great Grandparents:

Ruth the Moabite and Boaz the son of Rahab

Grandpa:

Obed

Dad:

Jesse

ANOINTED
To Suffer · To Serve · To Save

7 Also the cow and the bear will graze,
   Their young will lie down together,
   And the lion will eat straw like the ox.

8 The nursing child will play by the hole of the cobra,
   And the weaned child will put his hand on the viper's den.

9 They will not hurt or destroy in all My holy mountain,
   For the earth will be full of the knowledge of the LORD
   As the waters cover the sea.

10 Then in that day
   The nations will resort to the root of Jesse,
   Who will stand as a signal for the peoples;
   And His resting place will be glorious.

ONE STEP FURTHER:

Practice It

Without looking at the previous page or at your Bible, see how much of Isaiah 53:1-2 you can fill in below.

Who has believed our

And to whom has the

He grew up before Him as

And like a

He has no stately form or majesty that we should

Nor appearance that we should

Easier than you thought, right?! Keep up the great work!

DISCUSS with your GROUP or PONDER on your own . . .

According to 2 Samuel 7:13, what does God promise to do for David after he dies?

What will it take to establish a forever kingdom?

Isaiah 11:1 refers to the stem of Jesse. Who do you think that is referring to? Explain.

What do we learn about "the shoot"/"the branch" in Isaiah 11?

ANOINTED
TO SUFFER · TO SERVE · TO SAVE

How does it compare with "the shoot"/"root" in Isaiah 53?

What happens under the reign of "the shoot"/"the branch" in Isaiah 11? Has the world ever seen anything like this yet? What does this say about the timing of the prophecy?

If you were expecting a forever kingdom of peace, how do you think the idea of a suffering deliverer would strike you? Would you have believed the message? Explain.

More of the story . . . nothing that looks like fulfillment

The deliverance that God reveals in the tender shoot looks nothing like what the people would have anticipated. Let's look at our main text for the week once again.

OBSERVE the TEXT of SCRIPTURE

READ Isaiah 53:1-2 and **UNDERLINE** words and phrases associated with the Servant's appearance.

Isaiah 53:1-2

1 *Who has believed our message?*
   And to whom has the arm of the LORD been revealed?

2 *For He grew up before Him like a tender shoot,*
   And like a root out of parched ground;
   He has no stately form or majesty
   That we should look upon Him,
   Nor appearance that we should be attracted to Him.

ANOINTED
TO SUFFER · TO SERVE · TO SAVE

DISCUSS with your GROUP or PONDER on your own . . .

What type of environment does the Servant grow up in?

ONE STEP FURTHER:

Nothing Majestic

If you have time, look at the word "majesty" (Hebrew: *hadar*) in Isaiah 53:2. Note how the word is typically used in Isaiah and the rest of the Old Testament. Who is usually associated with "majesty"?

What do we learn about His physical appearance?

Is there anything about Him that seems extraordinary or attractive? Explain.

What do you usually look for in a hero or deliverer? What attributes does the current secular culture elevate? How do these qualities compare with the Servant's description?

More of the story . . . it has to be revealed

Nothing in outward appearance tipped off who the Servant was. Those who believe—then and now—believe because God reveals truth. Let's take a look at the Gospel of John where the evangelist clearly defines the Servant as Jesus Christ. As we pick up the narrative, Jesus has just raised Lazarus from the dead (John 11) and now predicts His own death (John 12).

OBSERVE the TEXT of SCRIPTURE

READ John 12:27-43 and **MARK** references to *Jesus*, including pronouns.

John 12:27-43

27 *"Now My soul has become troubled; and what shall I say, 'Father, save Me from this hour'? But for this purpose I came to this hour.*

28 "Father, glorify Your name." Then a voice came out of heaven: "I have both glorified it, and will glorify it again."

29 So the crowd of people *who stood by and heard it were* saying that it had thundered; others were saying, "An angel has spoken to Him."

30 Jesus answered and said, "This voice has not come for My sake, but for your sakes.

31 "Now judgment is upon this world; now the ruler of this world will be cast out.

32 "And I, if I am lifted up from the earth, will draw all men to Myself."

33 But He was saying this to indicate the kind of death by which He was to die.

34 The crowd then answered Him, "We have heard out of the Law that the Christ is to remain forever; and how can You say, 'The Son of Man must be lifted up'? Who is this Son of Man?"

35 So Jesus said to them, "For a little while longer the Light is among you. Walk while you have the Light, so that darkness will not overtake you; he who walks in the darkness does not know where he goes.

36 "While you have the Light, believe in the Light, so that you may become sons of Light." These things Jesus spoke, and He went away and hid Himself from them.

37 But though He had performed so many signs before them, yet they were not believing in Him.

38 This was to fulfill the word of Isaiah the prophet which he spoke: "LORD, WHO HAS BELIEVED OUR REPORT? AND TO WHOM HAS THE ARM OF THE LORD BEEN REVEALED?"

39 For this reason they could not believe, for Isaiah said again,

40 "HE HAS BLINDED THEIR EYES AND HE HARDENED THEIR HEART, SO THAT THEY WOULD NOT SEE WITH THEIR EYES AND PERCEIVE WITH THEIR HEART, AND BE CONVERTED AND I HEAL THEM."

41 These things Isaiah said because he saw His glory, and he spoke of Him.

42 Nevertheless many even of the rulers believed in Him, but because of the Pharisees they were not confessing Him, for fear that they would be put out of the synagogue;

43 for they loved the approval of men rather than the approval of God.

DISCUSS with your GROUP or PONDER on your own . . .

What do we learn about Jesus in John 12:27-43? You might want to make a simple list.

FYI:

Revealed!

13 "Now when Jesus came into the district of Caesarea Philippi, He was asking His disciples, "Who do people say that the Son of Man is?"

14 And they said, "Some say John the Baptist; and others, Elijah; but still others, Jeremiah, or one of the prophets."

15 He said to them, "But who do you say that I am?"

16 Simon Peter answered, "You are the Christ, the Son of the living God."

17 And Jesus said to him, "Blessed are you, Simon Barjona, because flesh and blood did not reveal this to you, but My Father who is in heaven."

—Matthew 16:13-17

ANOINTED
TO SUFFER · TO SERVE · TO SAVE

Lesson Two: **Who Has Believed? Have You?**

What questions does the crowd ask Jesus when He predicts His death? How does He respond?

Who believed the message? Who did not? Why?

@THE END OF THE DAY . . .

The question *Who has believed our message?* is as valid today as the day God first asked it. It is the one question on which the difference between life and death hangs.

Have *you* believed the message? Do *you* know the message well enough to share it with others?

If your answer to either of these questions is "no," what questions do you have that you need answered? What do you need to know better so you can share the good news of Jesus with others? Please don't skip answering these questions or rush through them casually. Take some time to sit quietly with God and ask Him to search your heart as you answer and to continue to work in your heart as we further plumb the depths of Isaiah 53!

LESSON THREE
Despised and Forsaken

*"We ourselves esteemed Him stricken, smitten of God,
and afflicted."*
–Isaiah 53:4b

Sorrow and grief mark the fallen human experience. No one escapes. When sin entered the world, death followed at its heels bringing to mankind pain and every imaginable suffering. Those who have believed the message about God's Servant, though, know they have a sorrow-bearer. Jesus, the perfect Servant of the LORD, entered into our sufferings and brokenness and lifted the weight from our weary shoulders.

God's perfect Servant was "made like His brethren in all things, so that He might become a merciful and faithful high priest in things pertaining to God, to make propitiation for the sins of the people" (Hebrews 2:17). Let's continue to look at the Servant this week in the pages of the New Testament. He can relate to those who are despised, forsaken, and ill-esteemed, because He, too, trod that path.

ANOINTED
TO SUFFER · TO SERVE · TO SAVE

Lesson Three: **Despised and Forsaken**

REMEMBERING

Take a few minutes to summarize what you learned last week.

What truth(s) have you been most actively applying?

If you memorized Isaiah 53:1-2, try to write it out from memory. If you didn't, no worries!

FYI:

Close to My Heart

People often ask me: "How do you decide what topics to write about?" The short answer is that I seek God and watch to see where He prompts me. Often it's a personal issue that needs to be addressed in my life—that's where *No Worries!* and *Sweeter than Chocolate! 1 Corinthians 13* came from. Other times it's a passion for deeply knowing God's Word that I'm compelled to share with others—enter *Sweeter than Chocolate! Psalm 119* and *Cookies on the Lower Shelf.*

This study is so close to my heart because I have Jewish friends in my life who I love, but who I know that God loves even more! In writing this, my heart has been to understand my Savior better and to understand how to share Him better with both my Jewish and non-Jewish friends. As I've been writing, I've tried to get into the mind, in a sense, of someone who does not come to Isaiah 53 assuming that the Servant is Jesus, to try to understand the questions that arise from that perspective in order to be able to relate and communicate better.

As I've been studying, though, so much more happens as the Spirit works. I've been struck personally by the fellowship of His suffering. There is nothing we face, nothing we endure, nothing we fear, that He does not understand and that He cannot heal.

WEEKLY OBSERVATION

We'll keep all of Isaiah 53 in front of us from week to week as we dive deeper into the text verse by verse.

OBSERVE the TEXT of SCRIPTURE

READ Isaiah 53 and **UNDERLINE** references to the Servant being *despised* and *forsaken*. Include any words and phrases that are synonyms.

Isaiah 53

1   Who has believed our message?
    And to whom has the arm of the LORD been revealed?

2   For He grew up before Him like a tender shoot,
    And like a root out of parched ground;
    He has no stately form or majesty
    That we should look upon Him,
    Nor appearance that we should be attracted to Him.

3   He was despised and forsaken of men,
    A man of sorrows and acquainted with grief;
    And like one from whom men hide their face
    He was despised, and we did not esteem Him.

4   Surely our griefs He Himself bore,
    And our sorrows He carried;
    Yet we ourselves esteemed Him stricken,
    Smitten of God, and afflicted.

5   But He was pierced through for our transgressions,
    He was crushed for our iniquities;
    The chastening for our well-being fell upon Him,
    And by His scourging we are healed.

6   All of us like sheep have gone astray,
    Each of us has turned to his own way;
    But the LORD has caused the iniquity of us all
    To fall on Him.

7   He was oppressed and He was afflicted,
    Yet He did not open His mouth;
    Like a lamb that is led to slaughter,
    And like a sheep that is silent before its shearers,
    So He did not open His mouth.

8   By oppression and judgment He was taken away;
    And as for His generation, who considered
    That He was cut off out of the land of the living
    For the transgression of my people, to whom the stroke was due?

9   His grave was assigned with wicked men,
    Yet He was with a rich man in His death,
    Because He had done no violence,
    Nor was there any deceit in His mouth.

10 But the LORD was pleased
    To crush Him, putting Him to grief;
    If He would render Himself as a guilt offering,
    He will see His offspring,
    He will prolong His days,
    And the good pleasure of the LORD will prosper in His hand.

11 As a result of the anguish of His soul,
    He will see it and be satisfied;
    By His knowledge the Righteous One,
    My Servant, will justify the many,
    As He will bear their iniquities.

12 Therefore, I will allot Him a portion with the great,
    And He will divide the booty with the strong;
    Because He poured out Himself to death,
    And was numbered with the transgressors;
    Yet He Himself bore the sin of many,
    And interceded for the transgressors.

FYI:

Remember to Pray
Just a quick reminder. If you're trying to do this alone, it will be much harder! Ask God to teach you through His Word as He taught the psalmist who prayed these words: "I have not turned aside from Your ordinances, for You Yourself have taught me" (Psalm 119:102). What an opportunity . . . to be taught by God!

ANOINTED
TO SUFFER · TO SERVE · TO SAVE

Lesson Three: **Despised and Forsaken**

DISCUSS with your GROUP or PONDER on your own . . .

Look back at where you marked references to the Servant being despised and forsaken. Make a simple list of those who despised Him and why.

LOOKING CLOSER . . .

As we focus on Isaiah 53:3-4 this week, we'll spend much of our time in the New Testament seeing how Jesus' life matches up with these prophecies. We'll also consider how He can sympathize better than anyone with our own pain and suffering.

OBSERVE the TEXT of SCRIPTURE

READ Isaiah 53:3-4 and **MARK** in a distinctive way any pairs of word you notice. For example, *despised* appears in lines 1 and 4 of verse 3.

Isaiah 53:3-4

3 *He was despised and forsaken of men,*
    A man of sorrows and acquainted with grief;
    And like one from whom men hide their face
    He was despised, and we did not esteem Him.

4 *Surely our griefs He Himself bore,*
    And our sorrows He carried;
    Yet we ourselves esteemed Him stricken,
    Smitten of God, and afflicted.

DISCUSS with your GROUP or PONDER on your own . . .

What repeating pairs of words did you see? What did you learn from each repeated pair?

1.

2.

3.

4.

What is the Servant's relationship to the speaker? What does He do for the speaker and his people?

Are there sorrows and griefs you need to let Jesus carry for you today? How does trying to carry them yourself affect you?

FYI:

Any good from Nazareth?

Philip found Nathanael and said to him, "We have found Him of whom Moses in the Law and also the Prophets wrote— Jesus of Nazareth, the son of Joseph." Nathanael said to him, "Can any good thing come out of Nazareth?" Philip said to him, "Come and see."

—John 1:45-46

FYI:

What do you do with your pain?

This week one of our family members faced a difficult betrayal. The pain has had a ripple effect and based on the situation, I know it is not long before the grief will strike others, too. The pain, the grief, the sorrow we are feeling—some of us first-hand, others second-hand—is a result of the collateral damage of sin. In the midst of it, the Spirit has been reminding me that I have One who has carried my grief and my sorrow; I never walk alone. There is One who not only understands, but has paid the price that we may be forgiven and made whole again. The only way that I can deal with pain is by running into the arms of the One who has given everything to heal it.

ANOINTED
To Suffer · To Serve · To Save

More of the story . . . looking to the New Testament

While His disciples loved Him and the masses followed Him, Jesus faced opposition and rejection from His earliest days. He is a Savior who knows your suffering and your pain intimately. Let's take a look at some of those who came against Him.

OBSERVE the TEXT of SCRIPTURE

Shortly after Jesus' birth, Magi from the east arrive to worship Him. We'll pick up the account after the local ruler, King Herod, realizes the Magi have left the country without disclosing the Child's location to him.

READ Matthew 2:16-23. **MARK** references to *Herod* (including pronouns) and **UNDERLINE** everything he does.

Matthew 2:16-23

16　*Then when Herod saw that he had been tricked by the magi, he became very enraged, and sent and slew all the male children who were in Bethlehem and all its vicinity, from two years old and under, according to the time which he had determined from the magi.*

17　*Then what had been spoken through Jeremiah the prophet was fulfilled:*

18　*"A VOICE WAS HEARD IN RAMAH, WEEPING AND GREAT MOURNING, RACHEL WEEPING FOR HER CHILDREN; AND SHE REFUSED TO BE COMFORTED, BECAUSE THEY WERE NO MORE."*

19　*But when Herod died, behold, an angel of the Lord appeared in a dream to Joseph in Egypt, and said,*

20　*"Get up, take the Child and His mother, and go into the land of Israel; for those who sought the Child's life are dead."*

21　*So Joseph got up, took the Child and His mother, and came into the land of Israel.*

22　*But when he heard that Archelaus was reigning over Judea in place of his father Herod, he was afraid to go there. Then after being warned by God in a dream, he left for the regions of Galilee,*

23　*and came and lived in a city called Nazareth. This was to fulfill what was spoken through the prophets: "He shall be called a Nazarene."*

DISCUSS with your GROUP or PONDER on your own . . .

Describe Herod from the text. Who is he? What does he do? Why does he despise Jesus?

How does God intervene to protect Jesus from Herod?

ONE STEP FURTHER:

Word Studies: "Despised" and "Forsaken"

If you have time this week, see if you can identify and explore the Hebrew words translated "despised" and "forsaken." Remember to pay closest attention to other uses in Isaiah (if applicable) and then see how the words are used in the rest of the Old Testament. Record what you discover below.

Despised:

Forsaken:

How long does the threat last and what does Joseph do about it? Why?

You may not be able to relate personally to such a threat coming against you or a family member—or maybe you can. Either way, we see that Jesus knew opposition from the earliest days.

FYI:

Hometowns
While Jesus grew up in Nazareth, southwest of the Sea of Galilee, His adopted hometown as an adult was the seaside city of Capernaum (Matthew 4:13), about 20 miles away.

OBSERVE the TEXT of SCRIPTURE

After escaping Herod's infanticide and spending subsequent time in Egypt, Jesus grows up in Nazareth. Mark 6:1-6 (with a parallel account in Matthew 13:54-58) records Jesus' rejection by the people in his hometown.

READ Mark 6:1-6 and **MARK** references to listeners in His "hometown," including pronouns.

Mark 6:1-6

1 *Jesus went out from there and came into His hometown; and His disciples followed Him.*

2 *When the Sabbath came, He began to teach in the synagogue; and the many listeners were astonished, saying, "Where did this man get these things, and what is this wisdom given to Him, and such miracles as these performed by His hands?*

3 *"Is not this the carpenter, the son of Mary, and brother of James and Joses and Judas and Simon? Are not His sisters here with us?" And they took offense at Him.*

4 *Jesus said to them, "A prophet is not without honor except in his hometown and among his own relatives and in his own household."*

5 *And He could do no miracle there except that He laid His hands on a few sick people and healed them.*

6 *And He wondered at their unbelief. And He was going around the villages teaching.*

DISCUSS with your GROUP or PONDER on your own . . .

How do the "many listeners" react to Jesus? How do they view Him?

What does Jesus say about them?

ANOINTED
To Suffer · To Serve · To Save

Has anyone close to you ever taken offense at you because of Jesus? How did you respond in the situation? How can the truth that those close to Jesus took offense at Him comfort you? What can you learn from Him?

ONE STEP FURTHER:

Offended!

If you have some extra time this week, pick a Gospel (Matthew, Mark, Luke, or John) and scan through it to see the different ways the religious leaders took offense at and despised Jesus. Record your observations below.

OBSERVE the TEXT of SCRIPTURE

John 7 records Jesus' ministry in the northern region of Galilee because of Jewish threats in the southern area of Judea.

READ John 7:1-8 and **MARK** references to "hatred" (*seeking to kill, hate*, etc.).

John 7:1-8

1 *After these things Jesus was walking in Galilee, for He was unwilling to walk in Judea because the Jews were seeking to kill Him.*

2 *Now the feast of the Jews, the Feast of Booths, was near.*

3 *Therefore His brothers said to Him, "Leave here and go into Judea, so that Your disciples also may see Your works which You are doing.*

4 *"For no one does anything in secret when he himself seeks to be* known *publicly. If You do these things, show Yourself to the world."*

5 *For not even His brothers were believing in Him.*

6 *So Jesus said to them, "My time is not yet here, but your time is always opportune.*

7 *"The world cannot hate you, but it hates Me because I testify of it, that its deeds are evil.*

8 *"Go up to the feast yourselves; I do not go up to this feast because My time has not yet fully come."*

DISCUSS with your GROUP or PONDER on your own . . .

What different groups of people are mentioned in this section? How does each relate to/view Jesus?

Why does Jesus say the world hates Him?

What can we expect if we stand up for truth in an age of evil?

Have you experienced the world's hatred because you've stood for truth? How can knowing what Jesus said help when hatred comes your way? How should you respond?

OBSERVE the TEXT of SCRIPTURE

As we've seen in the passages we've looked at thus far, Jesus experienced opposition throughout His life. Speaking to His disciples in what is often referred to as the Upper Room Discourse (John 15–17), Jesus warns them about the hate they will face because of Him after He's gone.

READ John 15:18-27 and **MARK** in a distinctive way, *world, hate* and *persecute*.

John 15:18-27

18 *"If the world hates you, you know that it has hated Me before* it hated you.

19 *"If you were of the world, the world would love its own; but because you are not of the world, but I chose you out of the world, because of this the world hates you.*

20 *"Remember the word that I said to you, 'A slave is not greater than his master.' If they persecuted Me, they will also persecute you; if they kept My word, they will keep yours also.*

21 *"But all these things they will do to you for My name's sake, because they do not know the One who sent Me.*

22 *"If I had not come and spoken to them, they would not have sin, but now they have no excuse for their sin.*

23 *"He who hates Me hates My Father also.*

24 *"If I had not done among them the works which no one else did, they would not have sin; but now they have both seen and hated Me and My Father as well.*

25 *"But they have done this to fulfill the word that is written in their Law, 'THEY HATED ME WITHOUT A CAUSE.'*

26 *"When the Helper comes, whom I will send to you from the Father, that is the Spirit of truth who proceeds from the Father, He will testify about Me,*

27 *and you will testify also, because you have been with Me from the beginning.*

ANOINTED
TO SUFFER · TO SERVE · TO SAVE

Lesson Three: **Despised and Forsaken**

DISCUSS with your GROUP or PONDER on your own . . .

What does Jesus warn His disciples about the world?

ONE STEP FURTHER:

Word Studies: "Sorrows" and "Griefs"

Take a little more time (if you have it!) to search out the Hebrew words translated "sorrows" and "griefs." Again, identify how else they are used in Isaiah and then take a look at how they are translated elsewhere in the Old Testament. Record your findings below.

Sorrows

Have you experienced this? Explain.

According to Jesus, why did the world hate him? Why will they hate us?

What does Jesus say about persecution?

Griefs

Who does the world love? What temptation does that pose to us? How can we stand?

OBSERVE the TEXT of SCRIPTURE

As you read Matthew's account of Jesus healing Peter's mother-in-law, note how he ties it to the fulfillment of Isaiah's prophecy.

READ Matthew 8:14-17 and **MARK** the word *sick*, including synonyms.

Matthew 8:14-17

14 *When Jesus came into Peter's home, He saw his mother-in-law lying sick in bed with a fever.*

ANOINTED
TO SUFFER · TO SERVE · TO SAVE

15 He touched her hand, and the fever left her; and she got up and waited on Him.

16 When evening came, they brought to Him many who were demon-possessed; and He cast out the spirits with a word, and healed all who were ill.

17 This was to fulfill what was spoken through Isaiah the prophet: "HE HIMSELF TOOK OUR INFIRMITIES AND CARRIED AWAY OUR DISEASES."

DISCUSS with your GROUP or PONDER on your own . . .

What situation does Jesus face at Peter's house? What does He do for Peter's mother-in-law?

What else does Jesus do while he is at the house?

How does Matthew say this fulfills Isaiah's prophecy?

Based on Matthew's interpretation of Isaiah, in what way do you think Jesus was a man of sorrows and acquainted with grief?

ONE STEP FURTHER:

John 11

If you have time this week, read John 11—the account of the sickness, death, and resurrection of Lazarus—keeping in mind the prophecy that the Servant would bear our griefs and carry our sorrows. Then record your observations below.

ANOINTED
TO SUFFER · TO SERVE · TO SAVE

Digging Deeper

Let's Memorize. . . Isaiah 53:3-4

There are myriad ways to memorize. One strategy that I often use is to watch for parallel phrases or repetitions in the text. I've broken the text apart in a way that helps me to see some repetitions and I hope it will help you, too.

Note that often the second line of a phrase repeats the same content as the first with slightly different words.

Verse 3

He was	***despised***	
	and	
	forsaken	of men

A man of	***sorrows***
	and
acquainted with	***grief;***

And like one from whom men hide their face

He was	***despised,***	
	and	
we did	***not esteem***	Him.

Verse 4

Surely	***our griefs***	*He* Himself ***bore,***
	And	
	our sorrows	*He carried;*

Yet we ourselves	***esteemed*** Him	***stricken***,
		smitten of God,
		and
		afflicted.

_____

• As you memorize, watch the repetition of the phrase "He was despised."
• Note that the "man of sorrows" (v. 3) carried our sorrows (v. 4).
• Similarly the man "acquainted with grief" (v. 3) bore our griefs (v. 4).
• In verse 3, "we did not esteem Him," but in verse 4 we "esteemed Him" badly, that is we esteemed Him "stricken, smitten of God, and afflicted."

_____

@THE END OF THE DAY . . .

As we wrap up our lesson, take a moment to ask God to search your heart. You may want to close the book and go take a walk as you do this. I'm equally guilty at times of thinking things are either too big or too small to bring to God. Neither, of course, is true.

Remember, this is the God who knows exactly how many hairs are on your head. He is the God who feeds the sparrows. Bring before Him any situations in life that, if you're honest, you've been trying to muscle through on your own power or maybe trying to stuff down out of sight.

Then look back over the lesson and consider the depth to which Jesus understands everything you are going through—every offense, every rejection, every instance of suffering. You are not alone. You have a Healer!

Lesson Three: **Despised and Forsaken**

LESSON FOUR
Crushed for Our Iniquities

". . . He was crushed for our iniquities . . ."
–Isaiah 53:5

Not fair! When we were kids we yelled it at each other and as adults the belief that we've gotten a raw deal for whatever reason often smolders in our memories. There is little we consider worse to us than believing that somehow we've gotten a raw deal, that life has not been fair.

As we look to Isaiah 53 this week, we will see the height of "unfair" when the perfect Servant bears others' sins and yet *brings them healing*.

Friends, "fair" for sinners according to God's standard of perfect justice is death and hell. What wonder, what mercy, what love that Jesus, the Servant of the LORD, did not give us "fair." Rather, He suffered for us, embracing our punishment to heal us and restore us to peace with God.

REMEMBERING

Take a few minutes to summarize what you learned last week.

What truth(s) have you been most actively applying?

Try to write out Isaiah 53:1-2 from memory. If you haven't memorized it word-for-word, at least write down the main ideas.

Now try Isaiah 53:3-4.

WEEKLY OBSERVATION

Again, since the core of our study is just 12 verses, we'll keep all of Isaiah 53 in front of us each week as we dive deeper into the text verse-by-verse.

OBSERVE the TEXT of SCRIPTURE

READ Isaiah 53 and **MARK** references to the Servant's physical suffering.

Isaiah 53

1   Who has believed our message?
     And to whom has the arm of the LORD been revealed?

2   For He grew up before Him like a tender shoot,
      And like a root out of parched ground;
      He has no stately form or majesty
      That we should look upon Him,
      Nor appearance that we should be attracted to Him.

3   He was despised and forsaken of men,
      A man of sorrows and acquainted with grief;
      And like one from whom men hide their face
      He was despised, and we did not esteem Him.

4   Surely our griefs He Himself bore,
      And our sorrows He carried;
      Yet we ourselves esteemed Him stricken,
      Smitten of God, and afflicted.

5   But He was pierced through for our transgressions,
      He was crushed for our iniquities;
      The chastening for our well-being fell upon Him,
      And by His scourging we are healed.

6   All of us like sheep have gone astray,
      Each of us has turned to his own way;
      But the LORD has caused the iniquity of us all
      To fall on Him.

7   He was oppressed and He was afflicted,
      Yet He did not open His mouth;
      Like a lamb that is led to slaughter,
      And like a sheep that is silent before its shearers,
      So He did not open His mouth.

8   By oppression and judgment He was taken away;
      And as for His generation, who considered
      That He was cut off out of the land of the living
      For the transgression of my people, to whom the stroke was due?

9   His grave was assigned with wicked men,
      Yet He was with a rich man in His death,
      Because He had done no violence,
      Nor was there any deceit in His mouth.

10 But the LORD was pleased
      To crush Him, putting Him to grief;
      If He would render Himself as a guilt offering,
      He will see His offspring,
      He will prolong His days,
      And the good pleasure of the LORD will prosper in His hand.

11 As a result of the anguish of His soul,
      He will see it and be satisfied;
      By His knowledge the Righteous One,
      My Servant, will justify the many,
      As He will bear their iniquities.

ONE STEP FURTHER:

Other Translations

If you have some extra time this week, you may want to read Isaiah 53 in a couple of other versions. If you do, write down the versions you used and record some of the variations that you saw. Remember, the NASB, the ESV, and the NKJV provide solid word-for-word translations from the original languages. Other versions that we sometimes deem "easier" to read are so because the translators have done interpretive work for us that may or may not be correct. Easier may seem helpful, but easy doesn't necessarily equal accurate. You'll understand clearly what the translator *thinks* the texts means, but what the text actually means may be obscured.

ANOINTED
To Suffer · To Serve · To Save

12 Therefore, I will allot Him a portion with the great,
    And He will divide the booty with the strong;
    Because He poured out Himself to death,
    And was numbered with the transgressors;
    Yet He Himself bore the sin of many,
    And interceded for the transgressors.

DISCUSS with your GROUP or PONDER on your own . . .

Look back at where you marked references to the Servant's suffering. Make a simple list of what He endured and from whom.

LOOKING CLOSER . . .

As we focus on Isaiah 53:5-6 this week, we'll again spend much of our time comparing the text to New Testament accounts of Jesus.

OBSERVE the TEXT of SCRIPTURE

READ Isaiah 53:5-6 and **MARK** in a distinctive way references to the Servant (*He, Him*), the LORD, and the transgressors (the first-person plural pronouns—*our, we, us*).

Isaiah 53:5-6

5 But He was pierced through for our transgressions,
   He was crushed for our iniquities;
   The chastening for our well-being fell upon Him,
   And by His scourging we are healed.

6 All of us like sheep have gone astray,
   Each of us has turned to his own way;
   But the LORD has caused the iniquity of us all
   To fall on Him.

ONE STEP FURTHER:

Word Studies: What the Servant Suffered

Isaiah 53:5-6 describes the suffering that the Servant endured in bringing well-being and healing to sinners like us. If you have time this week, use Blueletterbible.com to find the Hebrew words translated by each of the words below and see how these terms are used in Isaiah and throughout the Old Testament. Then record your findings below.

Pierced through:

Crushed:

Chastened:

Scourged:

ANOINTED
TO SUFFER · TO SERVE · TO SAVE

DISCUSS with your GROUP or PONDER on your own . . .

Now that you've marked the key words, go back and underline any other words associated with each. Once you've done that, summarize your findings in the chart below. I'll get you started:

The Servant:

• was pierced

What "we" bring to the table:

• transgressions

The LORD:

•

What "we" get in return:

•

What we deserved:

• to be pierced

FYI:

Using Commentaries
Commentaries are helpful tools after you've done your own study. You'll want to compare your findings with at least two or three authors to get balanced input.

FYI:

All Have Sinned
" . . . for all have sinned and fall short of the glory of God . . ."
—Romans 3:23

Although initially written to the Jewish people during the Isaiah's time, who else is included in the "our" and "us" of verses 5 and 6? As you think through this, consider Romans 3. Explain your answer.

Did the Servant do anything deserving of punishment or harsh treatment?

ANOINTED
To Suffer · To Serve · To Save

Lesson Four: **Crushed for Our Iniquities**

How do you typically respond when someone comes against you either for no reason or because you belong to Jesus? Does your attitude or response reflect how Jesus responded? If not, note changes you can make and how.

What is man's moral condition according to the text? Can you relate? In what way(s)?

How did the Servant fix this condition?

Given your answers above, what kind of well-being and healing do you think these verses are referring to?

Let's Compare Jesus . . .

Let's compare some facts about Jesus' death to the prophecy that we've just looked at and reason through the texts together. In the following passages we'll consider His innocence, His scourging, and His piercing

OBSERVE the TEXT of SCRIPTURE

READ Luke 18:31-34. In this passage Jesus speaks to his twelve disciples. **MARK** every reference to the *Son of Man* (including pronouns). **UNDERLINE** everything Jesus says will happen to the Son of Man.

Luke 18:31-34

31 *Then He took the twelve aside and said to them, "Behold, we are going up to Jerusalem, and all things which are written through the prophets about the Son of Man will be accomplished.*

ANOINTED
To Suffer · To Serve · To Save

32 "For He will be handed over to the Gentiles, and will be mocked and mistreated and spit upon,

33 and after they have scourged Him, they will kill Him; and the third day He will rise again."

34 But the disciples understood none of these things, and the meaning of this statement was hidden from them, and they did not comprehend the things that were said.

DISCUSS with your GROUP or PONDER on your own . . .

Who does the Son of Man refer to here? Explain your answer.

What was prophesied about Him? Compare what Jesus says here to Isaiah 53:5-6. Does it look like Jesus fulfilled the prophecy? Why/Why not?

Let's reason a little further. Did Jesus deserve anything that happened to Him? Given that, what can we learn from His example of suffering when He had done absolutely nothing wrong?

OBSERVE the TEXT of SCRIPTURE

READ Matthew 27:17-26 where the Jewish people are trying to persuade the Roman governor, Pilate, to crucify Jesus. **MARK** in a distinctive way every reference to *Jesus* (including synonyms and pronouns). Then **MARK** references to Pilate.

Matthew 27:17-26

17 So when the people gathered together, Pilate said to them, "Whom do you want me to release for you? Barabbas, or Jesus who is called Christ?"

18 For he knew that because of envy they had handed Him over.

19 While he was sitting on the judgment seat, his wife sent him a message, saying, "Have nothing to do with that righteous Man; for last night I suffered greatly in a dream because of Him."

20 But the chief priests and the elders persuaded the crowds to ask for Barabbas and to put Jesus to death.

ANOINTED
To Suffer · To Serve · To Save

Lesson Four: **Crushed for Our Iniquities**

21 But the governor said to them, "Which of the two do you want me to release for you?" And they said, "Barabbas."

22 Pilate said to them, "Then what shall I do with Jesus who is called Christ?" They all said, "Crucify Him!"

23 And he said, "Why, what evil has He done?" But they kept shouting all the more, saying, "Crucify Him!"

24 When Pilate saw that he was accomplishing nothing, but rather that a riot was starting, he took water and washed his hands in front of the crowd, saying, "I am innocent of this Man's blood; see to that yourselves."

25 And all the people said, "His blood shall be on us and on our children!"

26 Then he released Barabbas for them; but after having Jesus scourged, he handed Him over to be crucified.

ONE STEP FURTHER:

Word Study: "Christ"

"Christ" is not Jesus' last name! Take a few minutes this week to do a word study on "Christ." Using blueletterbible.org or another resource, see how the Greek word is used elsewhere in the New Testament and what the corresponding word is in Hebrew. What are the implications?

DISCUSS with your GROUP or PONDER on your own . . .

Look back at every place you marked references to Jesus. How is He referred to and by what people?

What did you learn about Pilate? What does he think about Jesus? What makes this situation difficult for him?

FYI:

His Blood is on My Hands and on Yours

In one of the most horrendous misinter-pretations/misapplications of Scripture, people calling themselves "Christians" have attempted to justify persecuting Jewish people on the basis of Matthew 27:25. Scripture clearly teaches that every person who has ever lived has sent Jesus to the cross—His blood, in essence, is on ALL of our hands but also that Jesus willingly chose to give Himself over on our behalf.

Who instigates this situation and why?

Is there any indication that Jesus is guilty? What happens to Him nonetheless? How does this compare to Isaiah 53:5-6?

ANOINTED
To Suffer · To Serve · To Save

44

OBSERVE the TEXT of SCRIPTURE

READ John 19:31-37 which takes place at Jesus' crucifixion. **MARK** the word *pierced*.

John 19:31-37

31 Then the Jews, because it was the day of preparation, so that the bodies would not remain on the cross on the Sabbath (for that Sabbath was a high day), asked Pilate that their legs might be broken, and that they might be taken away.

32 So the soldiers came, and broke the legs of the first man and of the other who was crucified with Him;

33 but coming to Jesus, when they saw that He was already dead, they did not break His legs.

34 But one of the soldiers pierced His side with a spear, and immediately blood and water came out.

35 And he who has seen has testified, and his testimony is true; and he knows that he is telling the truth, so that you also may believe.

36 For these things came to pass to fulfill the Scripture, "NOT A BONE OF HIM SHALL BE BROKEN."

37 And again another Scripture says, "THEY SHALL LOOK ON HIM WHOM THEY PIERCED."

DISCUSS with your GROUP or PONDER on your own . . .

What do the soldiers do to Jesus while He is still on the cross? How does this differ from the other men who were crucified? Why?

How does this text compare with what Isaiah prophesied in Isaiah 53?

What other prophecy does this text claim was fulfilled? (For more info on this, do the **One Step Further** section to the right!)

ONE STEP FURTHER:

No Broken Bones

Why would it matter that none of Jesus' bones were broken? I could tell you, but how much better if you find it yourself!

If you have time this week, read the following verses to answer the question for yourself and record below what you discover. The first reference below is a Messianic Psalm describing an incident in the life of David that points forward to something that will be fulfilled in the Messiah's life.

Psalm 34

Exodus 12:46

Numbers 9:12

Who or what is Jesus being compared to?

ANOINTED
TO SUFFER · TO SERVE · TO SAVE

Digging Deeper

Memorize It

Even if you decide not to try and memorize (although it would be great if you did!!), start training your brain to watch for text patterns. Below you can see some of the patterns that I've identified having to do with negatives and positives. Mark any additional patterns you noticed in the text.

Isaiah 53:5-6

5	But He was *pierced through*	for our transgressions, (negative action—rebellion against God)
	He was *crushed*	for our iniquities; (negative action)
	The *chastening*	for our well-being fell upon Him, (our positive outcome)
	And by His *scourging*	we are healed. (our positive outcome)

6	All of us like sheep	have gone astray,
	Each of us	has turned to his own way;
	(Repeating parallel statements)	
	But the LORD has caused the iniquity of us all	To fall on Him.
	(Expanded statement)	

I can only do so much with type. Use the space below to write out the verses in a way that can help you identify and remember the repetitions and parallelisms. Use color, size, spacing, etc. to help you encode and remember the content of the verses. Have fun!

ONE STEP FURTHER:

None Righteous

If you have time this week, read Romans 1–3 to see what the Apostle Paul says regarding the spiritual condition of all men. Pay attention to what he says about both Jewish and non-Jewish people. Record what you discover below.

More of the story . . . looking to the New Testament

We've looked at a number of passages that show Jesus' physical suffering. Now let's look at several more to find out how Jesus fits the profile of one who bears and forgives sins.

OBSERVE the TEXT of SCRIPTURE

As we pick up in Matthew 1, Joseph is planning to divorce Mary because of her pregnancy when he suddenly has an unexpected guest.

READ Matthew 1:20-24. **MARK** references to *Jesus* and **UNDERLINE** what He will do.

Matthew 1:20-24

20 *But when he had considered this, behold, an angel of the Lord appeared to him in a dream, saying, "Joseph, son of David, do not be afraid to take Mary as your wife; for the Child who has been conceived in her is of the Holy Spirit.*

21 *"She will bear a Son; and you shall call His name Jesus, for He will save His people from their sins."*

22 *Now all this took place to fulfill what was spoken by the Lord through the prophet:*

23 *"BEHOLD, THE VIRGIN SHALL BE WITH CHILD AND SHALL BEAR A SON, AND THEY SHALL CALL HIS NAME IMMANUEL," which translated means, "GOD WITH US."*

24 *And Joseph awoke from his sleep and did as the angel of the Lord commanded him, and took Mary as his wife,*

DISCUSS with your GROUP or PONDER on your own . . .

What does the angel of the Lord tell Joseph about Mary's Child?

How does Joseph respond? How does your obedience to God's revealed will compare with Joseph's in completeness and immediacy? Just asking.

FYI:

Four Accounts, One Life
The New Testament gives four separate accounts which paint a multi-faceted picture of Jesus' life, each from slightly different angles. New Testament scholars refer to Matthew, Mark, and Luke as the Synoptic (Greek: "together view") Gospels. Each disciple selects details of Jesus' life, teaching, and ministry for a different audience. Matthew writes to his Jewish brethren, Mark directs his words to the Roman mind, while Luke writes to "Theophilus," a proper name but also Greek for "God lover." John, by contrast, uses seven of Jesus' miracles to frame his gospel account to cause his readers to "believe that Jesus is the Christ, the Son of God," and that believing they "may have life in His name" (John 20:31).

ANOINTED
To Suffer · To Serve · To Save

Lesson Four: **Crushed for Our Iniquities**

OBSERVE the TEXT of SCRIPTURE

As John the Apostle opens his Gospel account, he introduces his readers to another famous John—John the Baptist—a man who baptizes in the wilderness saying that he is preparing the way of the Lord. As we pick up the story, John the Baptist declares who he has been preaching about.

READ John 1:29-45. **MARK** all references to *Jesus* (including synonyms and pronouns) and, again, **UNDERLINE** what He will do.

John 1:29-45

29 *The next day he* [John the Baptist] *saw Jesus coming to him and said, "Behold, the Lamb of God who takes away the sin of the world!*

30 *"This is He on behalf of whom I said, 'After me comes a Man who has a higher rank than I, for He existed before me.'*

31 *"I did not recognize Him, but so that He might be manifested to Israel, I came baptizing in water."*

32 *John testified saying, "I have seen the Spirit descending as a dove out of heaven, and He remained upon Him.*

33 *"I did not recognize Him, but He who sent me to baptize in water said to me, 'He upon whom you see the Spirit descending and remaining upon Him, this is the One who baptizes in the Holy Spirit.'*

34 *"I myself have seen, and have testified that this is the Son of God."*

35 *Again the next day John was standing with two of his disciples,*

36 *and he looked at Jesus as He walked, and said, "Behold, the Lamb of God!"*

37 *The two disciples heard him speak, and they followed Jesus.*

38 *And Jesus turned and saw them following, and said to them, "What do you seek?" They said to Him, "Rabbi (which translated means Teacher), where are You staying?"*

39 *He said to them, "Come, and you will see." So they came and saw where He was staying; and they stayed with Him that day, for it was about the tenth hour.*

40 *One of the two who heard John speak and followed Him, was Andrew, Simon Peter's brother.*

41 *He found first his own brother Simon and said to him, "We have found the Messiah" (which translated means Christ).*

42 *He brought him to Jesus. Jesus looked at him and said, "You are Simon the son of John; you shall be called Cephas" (which is translated Peter).*

43 *The next day He purposed to go into Galilee, and He found Philip. And Jesus said to him, "Follow Me."*

44 *Now Philip was from Bethsaida, of the city of Andrew and Peter.*

45 *Philip found Nathanael and said to him, "We have found Him of whom Moses in the Law and also the Prophets wrote—Jesus of Nazareth, the son of Joseph."*

DISCUSS with your GROUP or PONDER on your own . . .

How does John the Baptist describe Jesus? (What report/message does he give?)

What does John say that Jesus will do?

What connections would first-century Jewish people have made between a lamb and sin? (see Exodus 29:38ff, Numbers 28:3ff.)

What in the text indicates that the Jewish people were on the lookout for someone special? Who/what were they looking for and how did they know to look?

How did John know who Jesus was?

Who in this account believes John's report? What do they do as a result?

What additional titles do these believers attribute to Jesus?

Take a moment to consider each of the names/titles given to Jesus in John 1:29-49. Write down how your life reflects (or fails to reflect) the reality of each.

ANOINTED
To Suffer · To Serve · To Save

OBSERVE the TEXT of SCRIPTURE

As we pick up the text in Luke 5, Jesus is teaching and a large crowd is present.

READ Luke 5:17-26 and **MARK** *sin* and *forgive/forgiven*.

Luke 5:17-26

17 *One day He [Jesus]was teaching; and there were* some *Pharisees and teachers of the law sitting* there, *who had come from every village of Galilee and Judea and* from *Jerusalem; and the power of the Lord was* present *for Him to perform healing.*

18 *And* some *men were carrying on a bed a man who was paralyzed; and they were trying to bring him in and to set him down in front of Him.*

19 *But not finding any* way *to bring him in because of the crowd, they went up on the roof and let him down through the tiles with his stretcher, into the middle* of the crowd, *in front of Jesus.*

20 *Seeing their faith, He said, "Friend, your sins are forgiven you."*

21 *The scribes and the Pharisees began to reason, saying, "Who is this* man who *speaks blasphemies? Who can forgive sins, but God alone?"*

22 *But Jesus, aware of their reasonings, answered and said to them, "Why are you reasoning in your hearts?*

23 *"Which is easier, to say, 'Your sins have been forgiven you,' or to say, 'Get up and walk'?*

24 *"But, so that you may know that the Son of Man has authority on earth to forgive sins,"—He said to the paralytic—"I say to you, get up, and pick up your stretcher and go home."*

25 *Immediately he got up before them, and picked up what he had been lying on, and went home glorifying God.*

26 *They were all struck with astonishment and began glorifying God; and they were filled with fear, saying, "We have seen remarkable things today."*

DISCUSS with your GROUP or PONDER on your own . . .

Describe the situation Jesus is in. Where is He? Who is there? What is going on?

What do the men want Jesus to do? What lengths do they go to, to get it?

ONE STEP FURTHER:

Word Studies: What the Servant Suffered

While the Servant of the Lord suffers piercing, crushing, chastening, and scourging, it is not on account of anything He has done. Rather, it is for the sins *of others.* Take some time this week to explore the Hebrew words that are translated *transgressions, iniquities,* and *gone astray.* See what root they are from and how they compare to one another. Remember to note how they are used in both Isaiah and the rest of the Old Testament.

Trangressions:

Iniquities:

Gone astray:

What does Jesus do first instead?

Who gets upset and why? What do they realize about forgiveness?

What does Jesus eventually do for the paralyzed man? What does it show about Him?

Which do you think is the bigger miracle? Which is the more significant healing?

If you have experienced Christ's forgiveness, how has it changed your relationship with God?

How do you live as a forgiven person in your relationship with others? Does your life reflect your gratitude to God for having forgiven you?

@THE END OF THE DAY . . .

Take some time to ask God to reveal the extent to which you're living in the truth of His abundant forgiveness. If you're still beating yourself up over sins that Christ died to forgive, it's time to accept the forgiveness that He paid such a high price for and to move forward in freedom today! Will you do that? Will you help others to do the same?

ONE STEP FURTHER:

Well-being

Take just a couple of minutes this week to locate the Hebrew word for "well-being" and write it down. Even in Hebrew, you'll recognize it!!

ANOINTED
To Suffer · To Serve · To Save

Lesson Five: **Crushed for Our Iniquities**

LESSON FIVE
Bad Sheep and the Perfect Lamb

"Like a lamb that is led to slaughter,
And like a sheep that is silent before its shearers,
So He did not open His mouth."
–Isaiah 53:7

There is nothing like a redemption story line to make us weep. For most of us, a little piece of our heart died along the way with one fictional character or another who died an untimely death usually giving his (or her) life in some way for someone else. Perhaps your mind goes to Dickens' Sydney Carton. Others may think of Lewis's Aslan or Mufasa from the Lion King. More recently some Americans tear up at the mention of a crock-pot! Something touches us deeply when we encounter sacrifice, even in story.

Real-life sacrifice reaches even deeper. Isaiah 53 prophesies the greatest sacrifice account of all time as an innocent and perfect Lamb dies silently for brazen and straying sheep. Sometimes we forget both the horror and the wonder of Jesus' sacrifice on our behalf. LORD, forgive us and help us to see with fresh eyes and pliable hearts, the depth of Your sacrifice and Your love for sinners such as us.

REMEMBERING

Take a few minutes to summarize what you learned last week.

Hear, Apply, Remember, Repeat

I know it can be tempting to fly over application questions, especially review application questions! Please don't.

Jesus is clear that wise people not only hear His words but also act on them (Matthew 7:24-28). If we seek to act on what we hear and learn, it's critical that we take time to actively review and remember what God has said and what He has done.

Throughout the pages of Scripture we encounter over and over again people who "knew better" but then forgot. Let's learn from their example and resolve to not repeat their folly.

What truth(s) have you been most actively applying?

Try to write out Isaiah 53:1-4 from memory. If you haven't memorized it word-for-word, at least write down the main ideas.

Now try Isaiah 53:5-6.

WEEKLY OBSERVATION

Let's again start our week by reading and observing Isaiah 53!

OBSERVE the TEXT of SCRIPTURE

READ Isaiah 53 and **MARK** references to "our" culpability in the Servant's suffering.

Isaiah 53

1 *Who has believed our message?*
   And to whom has the arm of the LORD been revealed?

2 *For He grew up before Him like a tender shoot,*
   And like a root out of parched ground;
   He has no stately form or majesty
   That we should look upon Him,
   Nor appearance that we should be attracted to Him.

3 *He was despised and forsaken of men,*
   A man of sorrows and acquainted with grief;
   And like one from whom men hide their face
   He was despised, and we did not esteem Him.

4 *Surely our griefs He Himself bore,*
   And our sorrows He carried;
   Yet we ourselves esteemed Him stricken,
   Smitten of God, and afflicted.

5 *But He was pierced through for our transgressions,*
   He was crushed for our iniquities;
   The chastening for our well-being fell upon Him,
   And by His scourging we are healed.

6 *All of us like sheep have gone astray,*
   Each of us has turned to his own way;
   But the LORD has caused the iniquity of us all
   To fall on Him.

7 *He was oppressed and He was afflicted,*
   Yet He did not open His mouth;
   Like a lamb that is led to slaughter,
   And like a sheep that is silent before its shearers,
   So He did not open His mouth.

8 *By oppression and judgment He was taken away;*
   And as for His generation, who considered
   That He was cut off out of the land of the living
   For the transgression of my people, to whom the stroke was due?

9 *His grave was assigned with wicked men,*
   Yet He was with a rich man in His death,
   Because He had done no violence,
   Nor was there any deceit in His mouth.

ANOINTED
To Suffer · To Serve · To Save

55

10 *But the LORD was pleased*
To crush Him, putting Him to grief;
If He would render Himself as a guilt offering,
He will see His offspring,
He will prolong His days,
And the good pleasure of the LORD will prosper in His hand.

11 *As a result of the anguish of His soul,*
He will see it and be satisfied;
By His knowledge the Righteous One,
My Servant, will justify the many,
As He will bear their iniquities.

12 *Therefore, I will allot Him a portion with the great,*
And He will divide the booty with the strong;
Because He poured out Himself to death,
And was numbered with the transgressors;
Yet He Himself bore the sin of many,
And interceded for the transgressors.

DISCUSS with your GROUP or PONDER on your own . . .

Who is the "our" primarily referring to in Isaiah 53? Explain your answer.

Make a list noting what you learned from the text about "our" culpability in the Servant's suffering.

LOOKING CLOSER . . .

As we look more closely at the text this week, we'll pick up one of our verses from last week to see the full contrast between the bad and good sheep. So don't fret, it's not a mistake; we're overlapping on purpose!

OBSERVE the TEXT of SCRIPTURE

READ Isaiah 53:6-8 and **MARK** references to *sheep*, including pronouns. As you **MARK** make a distinction between the good sheep and the bad ones.

Isaiah 53:6-8

6 *All of us like sheep have gone astray,*
   Each of us has turned to his own way;
   But the LORD has caused the iniquity of us all
   To fall on Him.

7 *He was oppressed and He was afflicted,*
   Yet He did not open His mouth;
   Like a lamb that is led to slaughter,
   And like a sheep that is silent before its shearers,
   So He did not open His mouth.

8 *By oppression and judgment He was taken away;*
   And as for His generation, who considered
   That He was cut off out of the land of the living
   For the transgression of my people, to whom the stroke was due?

DISCUSS with your GROUP or PONDER on your own . . .

What "Who?" questions do we need to answer in verses 6 and 7?

> ## INDUCTIVE FOCUS:
>
> ### Who, What, When, Where, Why, and How
>
> Remember, when we ask the 5W and H questions, we'll often find there are several "Who?"s we have to look into, a number of "What?"s that grab our attention, and more than enough "When?"s, "Where?"s, "Why?"s, and "How?"s to keep us occupied for quite some time!

Looking to the New Testament

Let's look to the New Testament for some more insight into straying and sheep.

OBSERVE the TEXT of SCRIPTURE

We'll pick up this theme in the doctrinal letter of Romans where Paul builds the argument that all people stand condemned before God because of sin.

READ Romans 3:9-12 and **MARK** *all* and *none* references.

Romans 3:9-12

9 *What then? Are we better than they? Not at all; for we have already charged that both Jews and Greeks are all under sin;*

10 *as it is written, "THERE IS NONE RIGHTEOUS, NOT EVEN ONE;*

11 *THERE IS NONE WHO UNDERSTANDS, THERE IS NONE WHO SEEKS FOR GOD;*

12 *ALL HAVE TURNED ASIDE, TOGETHER THEY HAVE BECOME USELESS; THERE IS NONE WHO DOES GOOD, THERE IS NOT EVEN ONE."*

> ## FYI:
>
> ### Quoting the Psalms
>
> Paul makes his case in Romans 3 that everyone is under sin, adapting quotes from Psalm 14:1-3 and Psalm 53:1-3.

ANOINTED
TO SUFFER · TO SERVE · TO SAVE

DISCUSS with your GROUP or PONDER on your own . . .

What does Paul say about *all*? What have *all* done? How does he specifically define *all*?

ONE STEP FURTHER:

Get the Context!
If you have time this week, read Romans 1:18–3:20 to see Paul's argument for the condition of all mankind apart from God. Then record your observations below. Be sure to include his bottom-line position.

What did you learn by marking *none*?

Based on these verses, give a biblical definition of the human condition.

How do you think this compares with culture's view?

Now, a little closer to home: how does this compare with your view? Does what you say you believe match your behavior? Consider especially what the text says about people being "good."

If we view most people as "good," how will that affect our witness? Think it through and explain.

Even though the original audience of Isaiah 53 was Jewish, who else biblically fits the straying sheep profile? What implications does this have for all people?

OBSERVE the TEXT of SCRIPTURE

Now let's take some time to look at John 10 where Jesus talks about all of His sheep. Remember, we are cross-referencing to see if it will shed light on the straying sheep in Isaiah.

READ John 10:11-18 and **MARK** every reference to *sheep* and *shepherd* including pronouns.

John 10:11-18

11 *"I am the good shepherd; the good shepherd lays down His life for the sheep.*

12 *"He who is a hired hand, and not a shepherd, who is not the owner of the sheep, sees the wolf coming, and leaves the sheep and flees, and the wolf snatches them and scatters them.*

13 *"He flees because he is a hired hand and is not concerned about the sheep.*

14 *"I am the good shepherd, and I know My own and My own know Me,*

15 *even as the Father knows Me and I know the Father; and I lay down My life for the sheep.*

16 *"I have other sheep, which are not of this fold; I must bring them also, and they will hear My voice; and they will become one flock with one shepherd.*

17 *"For this reason the Father loves Me, because I lay down My life so that I may take it again.*

18 *"No one has taken it away from Me, but I lay it down on My own initiative. I have authority to lay it down, and I have authority to take it up again. This commandment I received from My Father."*

DISCUSS with your GROUP or PONDER on your own . . .

Who is the Good Shepherd and what do we learn about Him in John 10? This would be a great place to make a list.

ONE STEP FURTHER:

Jesus' View on "Good"
Take some time this week to find out what Jesus says with reference to goodness. You can locate this in any of the synoptic gospels: Matthew 19:16-30, Mark 10:17-31, or Luke 18:18-30. Unless you're a crazy over-achiever, just check one of the accounts and record below what you discover. How does your view match up with Jesus' view? Just asking.

Lesson Five: **Bad Sheep and the Perfect Lamb**

What does Jesus twice say that He does for the sheep?

What do we learn about His authority in verse 18? How does this relate to what He will undergo for His sheep?

What does Jesus say about His sheep?

How does this compare with Isaiah 53?

Who do you think the "other sheep" are? Why?

How will the "other sheep" and the original sheep be related to one another? What outcomes should accompany that?

How does Jesus' example of self-giving love encourage you? Does it scare you? If so, why?

Take some time to reflect on how being a recipient of this kind of love should impact how you treat others.

LOOKING CLOSER . . .

Let's go back to Isaiah 53:7-8 to focus on Jesus' response to oppression.

OBSERVE the TEXT of SCRIPTURE

READ Isaiah 53:7-8 in both the NASB and ESV translations. Then in both
UNDERLINE references to what the Servant endured (e.g. *oppressed, afflicted,* etc.)
CIRCLE or **HIGHLIGHT** the Servant's response.

Isaiah 53:7-8, NASB

7   *He was oppressed and He was afflicted,*
    Yet He did not open His mouth;
    Like a lamb that is led to slaughter,
    And like a sheep that is silent before its shearers,
    So He did not open His mouth.

8   *By oppression and judgment He was taken away;*
    And as for His generation, who considered
    That He was cut off out of the land of the living
    For the transgression of my people, to whom the stroke was due?

Isaiah 53:7-8, ESV

7   *He was oppressed, and he was afflicted,*
    yet he opened not his mouth;
    like a lamb that is led to the slaughter,
    and like a sheep that before its shearers is silent,
    so he opened not his mouth.

8   *By oppression and judgment he was taken away;*
    and as for his generation, who considered
    that he was cut off out of the land of the living,
    stricken for the transgression of my people?

ONE STEP FURTHER:

Following Jesus' Way
Take some time this week to see what Jesus says about following Him. Try using a concordance—either a book or online—to find your own references. Start off by thinking through what search terms will likely lead you to the results you need. Here are some that come to mind for me: "follow," "come after," "disciple." List your search words and then see what you learn. Record your finding below. Be sure to note the change that Jesus makes in those who follow Him!

ANOINTED
TO SUFFER · TO SERVE · TO SAVE

Lesson Five: **Bad Sheep and the Perfect Lamb**

DISCUSS with your GROUP or PONDER on your own . . .

What does the Servant endure? What is he compared to?

According to verse 8, how/why was the Servant taken away?

How does the Servant respond? How does this compare with the Gospel accounts? (See Matthew 27:11-14; Luke 23:12.)

What was the ultimate outcome? What happened to the Servant?

Who deserved "the stroke" that the Servant endured? Did anyone even consider this? Why do you think this is?

How often do you consider Jesus and what He suffered for you? What prompts you to consider? What tempts you to forget?

ONE STEP FURTHER:

Jeremiah's Response
If you have some extra time this week, see how Jeremiah responded when he faced plots against his life in Jeremiah 11:18-20. Record what you find below.

ANOINTED
TO SUFFER · TO SERVE · TO SAVE

Digging Deeper

The Crucifixion

Take some time this week to read the crucifixion account in each of the Gospels and record below what you observe and how it compares with Isaiah's prophecy.

Matthew

Mark

Luke

John

Summarize what you learned from the four accounts together. How do they compare with what you have seen in Isaiah 53?

FYI:

Fitting that One Man Die

Not unlike the Old Testament prophet Balaam, Caiaphas prophesies truth to a council made up of the chief priests and the Pharisees while simultaneously attempting to oppose God's plan.

We see this in John 11:49-52 right on the heels of Jesus raising Lazarus from the dead:

49 But one of them, Caiaphas, who was high priest that year, said to them, "You know nothing at all,

50 nor do you take into account that it is expedient for you that one man die for the people, and that the whole nation not perish."

51 Now he did not say this on his own initiative, but being high priest that year, he prophesied that Jesus was going to die for the nation,

52 and not for the nation only, but in order that He might also gather together into one the children of God who are scattered abroad.

ANOINTED
TO SUFFER · TO SERVE · TO SAVE

Lesson Five: **Bad Sheep and the Perfect Lamb**

OBSERVE the TEXT of SCRIPTURE

Before we finish off this week, let's explore why "considering Jesus" and what He has suffered on our behalf is so important. We'll pick up in Hebrews 12 which refers back to all the faithful witnesses recorded in the previous chapter.

READ Hebrews 12:1-3 and **MARK** every reference to *Jesus* including synonyms and pronouns.

Hebrews 12:1-3

1   Therefore, since we have so great a cloud of witnesses surrounding us, let us also lay aside every encumbrance and the sin which so easily entangles us, and let us run with endurance the race that is set before us,

2   fixing our eyes on Jesus, the author and perfecter of faith, who for the joy set before Him endured the cross, despising the shame, and has sat down at the right hand of the throne of God.

3   For consider Him who has endured such hostility by sinners against Himself, so that you will not grow weary and lose heart.

DISCUSS with your GROUP or PONDER on your own . . .

Who are we called to fix our eyes on? How is He described? What did He do?

Based on this description, do you think Jesus understands how you feel when people come against you? What difference can that make?

Do you ever grow weary and lose heart? If so, what prompts this?

How can considering Jesus help? What tangible benefits does considering Jesus bring?

Digging Deeper

Memorize It

Don't forget to keep up your memory work. This week we'll try to commit to memory Isaiah 53:7-8.

Write the verses below and identify key repeating phrases and patterns that can help you remember them. Use spacing, marking, etc. to help you see the structure of the verses more clearly.

Isaiah 53:7

Isaiah 53:8

@THE END OF THE DAY . . .

Take some time to think about how you can continually "consider Jesus," the perfect lamb, as you go about your day. Write down anything that the Lord brings to mind and ask Him to help you walk in obedience to His will and His way today.

LESSON SIX
No Violence, No Deceit

" . . . He had done no violence,
nor was there any deceit in His mouth."
–Isaiah 53:9b

By every human account, the Servant's death was a tragic miscarriage of justice. How could something so heinous happen? A complete innocent dying silently at the hands of evil men who first wrongly convict and then brutally torture Him!

As we'll see this week and next, while on the surface the Servant's suffering and death look like a tragic mistake, it was the high cost at the core of God's eternal plan to reconcile mankind to Himself. The free gift of salvation that God offers to you and me came at the highest cost to the Heavenly Father.

Lesson Six: **No Violence, No Deceit**

REMEMBERING

Take a few minutes to consider and write down one truth that God has most cemented to your heart thus far from Isaiah 53. How are you applying this truth today?

Try writing Isaiah 53:1-4 from memory. If you haven't memorized it word-for-word, write out the main ideas. That works, too!

FYI:

Use a Pencil!

When I'm doing memory work, I use an eraser—a big one! Writing out what you've memorized can be humbling the first time you try it, but as you repeat the process you'll start to remember the "misses" more and more and fill in the weak spots in your memory. Don't just trust me on this . . . try it!

FYI:

Harder Memorizing? Better Meditating!

I'm becoming more and more convinced that as memorizing becomes harder with aging, we become better at meditating. The simple reason? It takes longer to put it in and we have to actually think about what we're remembering so it will stick!

When I was younger, I could remember almost anything. I didn't need context and I didn't have to anchor memory to meaning. Most things would just stick if I applied any effort. In fact, I often memorized things without understanding at all!

continued on next page

Now try Isaiah 53:5-8.

WEEKLY OBSERVATION

Let's read through Isaiah 53 as we get started.

OBSERVE the TEXT of SCRIPTURE

READ Isaiah 53 and **MARK** any contrasts or comparisons that you note. This is a great place to use two different highlighters if you have them on hand—that's one option but remember, you rule the tools; don't let them rule you!

Isaiah 53

1   Who has believed our message?
    And to whom has the arm of the LORD been revealed?

2   For He grew up before Him like a tender shoot,
    And like a root out of parched ground;
    He has no stately form or majesty
    That we should look upon Him,
    Nor appearance that we should be attracted to Him.

3   He was despised and forsaken of men,
    A man of sorrows and acquainted with grief;
    And like one from whom men hide their face
    He was despised, and we did not esteem Him.

4   Surely our griefs He Himself bore,
    And our sorrows He carried;
    Yet we ourselves esteemed Him stricken,
    Smitten of God, and afflicted.

5   But He was pierced through for our transgressions,
    He was crushed for our iniquities;
    The chastening for our well-being fell upon Him,
    And by His scourging we are healed.

6   All of us like sheep have gone astray,
    Each of us has turned to his own way;
    But the LORD has caused the iniquity of us all
    To fall on Him.

7   He was oppressed and He was afflicted,
    Yet He did not open His mouth;
    Like a lamb that is led to slaughter,
    And like a sheep that is silent before its shearers,
    So He did not open His mouth.

8   By oppression and judgment He was taken away;
    And as for His generation, who considered
    That He was cut off out of the land of the living
    For the transgression of my people, to whom the stroke was due?

9   His grave was assigned with wicked men,
    Yet He was with a rich man in His death,
    Because He had done no violence,
    Nor was there any deceit in His mouth.

FYI:

Harder Memorizing? Better Meditating! (continued)

Among other things, I memorized my KJV Bible verses with the "Thee"s and "Thou"s and I memorized television jingles. In the early 1970s, the television station WGN promoted their comedy line-up using Stephen Sondheim's song *Comedy Tonight* (I just found this out today by Googling it!) that featured the lines:

Nothing with kings, nothing with crowns;
Bring on the lovers, liars and clowns!
Old situations, new complications,
Nothing portentous or polite; (these words are new to me . . . I sang something like "nothing for tents and all delight!")
Tragedy tomorrow (although my parents repeatedly corrected me, I persisted in singing "skagedy")
Comedy tonight!

Short story: I memorized words to a tune and had no idea what I was saying—even when corrected!

Now when I memorize, I think about what I'm trying to remembering. I slow down. I consider. I meditate. It takes longer, but it is so much more effective! I can't "just memorize" any more. To memorize now, I have to consider and think and meditate on the text!

Turns out aging isn't such a skagedy after all!

ANOINTED
TO SUFFER · TO SERVE · TO SAVE

Lesson Six: **No Violence, No Deceit**

10 But the LORD was pleased
   To crush Him, putting Him to grief;
   If He would render Himself as a guilt offering,
   He will see His offspring,
   He will prolong His days,
   And the good pleasure of the LORD will prosper in His hand.

11 As a result of the anguish of His soul,
   He will see it and be satisfied;
   By His knowledge the Righteous One,
   My Servant, will justify the many,
   As He will bear their iniquities.

12 Therefore, I will allot Him a portion with the great,
   And He will divide the booty with the strong;
   Because He poured out Himself to death,
   And was numbered with the transgressors;
   Yet He Himself bore the sin of many,
   And interceded for the transgressors.

DISCUSS with your GROUP or PONDER on your own . . .

What contrasts and comparisons did you note in the text?

How does the Servant compare/contrast with the people?

How does the Servant's earthly "start" compare/contrast with His "finish"?

LOOKING CLOSER . . .

Although the Servant's death is temporally tragic, God's eternal purpose for Him far exceeds man's wildest expectations.

OBSERVE the TEXT of SCRIPTURE

READ Isaiah 53:9-10 and **MARK** references (all pronouns) to *the Servant* and the *LORD.*

Isaiah 53:9-10

9　*His grave was assigned with wicked men,*
　　Yet He was with a rich man in His death,
　　Because He had done no violence,
　　Nor was there any deceit in His mouth.

10　*But the LORD was pleased*
　　To crush Him, putting Him to grief;
　　If He would render Himself as a guilt offering,
　　He will see His offspring,
　　He will prolong His days,
　　And the good pleasure of the LORD will prosper in His hand.

DISCUSS with your GROUP or PONDER on your own . . .

Let's make two simple lists to help us see everything we can about the Servant and the LORD in these verses.

The Servant　　　　　　　　　　The LORD

DISCUSS with your GROUP or PONDER on your own . . .

What contrasting circumstances surround the Servant's death in the first half of Isaiah 53:9? Who was He supposed to be with? Who did He end up with?

Digging Deeper

Let's Keep Memorizing . . .

Let's keep memorizing! Even if you're not reaching word-for-word accuracy, studying with recall as a goal will help you retain the main thoughts of the passage. We'll only do verse 9 this week!

9 *His grave was assigned with wicked men,*
   Yet He was with a rich man in His death,
   Because He had done no violence,
   Nor was there any deceit in His mouth.

Here are some of the words and patterns I noticed. Be sure to mark any others that you see.

9 *His* **grave** *was assigned with*   **wicked men,**

   Yet He was with a **rich man**   *in His* **death,**

   Because He had done   **no violence,**

   Nor *was there any* **deceit**   *in His mouth.*

Now, you take a turn identifying any other memory hooks that you see. Then write the verse down below in a form that helps you remember it.

OBSERVE the TEXT of SCRIPTURE

Let's take a look at a couple of passages about Jesus that show what happened to Him and why. The first tells us about the charges against Him, the second about the aftermath of the crucifixion.

READ Matthew 27:37-38 and John 19:31-37 and **MARK** distinctively references to the different people involved in the action. We have already looked at John 19 in Lesson 4, but we'll ask questions from another angle this time.

Matthew 27:37-38

37 And above His head they put up the charge against Him which read, *"THIS IS JESUS THE KING OF THE JEWS."*

38 At that time two robbers were crucified with Him, one on the right and one on the left.

John 19:31-37

31 Then the Jews, because it was the day of preparation, so that the bodies would not remain on the cross on the Sabbath (for that Sabbath was a high day), asked Pilate that their legs might be broken, and that they might be taken away.

32 So the soldiers came, and broke the legs of the first man and of the other who was crucified with Him;

33 but coming to Jesus, when they saw that He was already dead, they did not break His legs.

34 But one of the soldiers pierced His side with a spear, and immediately blood and water came out.

35 And he who has seen has testified, and his testimony is true; and he knows that he is telling the truth, so that you also may believe.

36 For these things came to pass to fulfill the Scripture, *"NOT A BONE OF HIM SHALL BE BROKEN."*

37 And again another Scripture says, *"THEY SHALL LOOK ON HIM WHOM THEY PIERCED."*

DISCUSS with your GROUP or PONDER on your own . . .

Who is being crucified and for what reasons?

Who wants the bodies removed from the crosses and why?

ANOINTED
To Suffer · To Serve · To Save

73

Who's in charge of what happens to the bodies? What does he permit to happen and why?

What do the soldiers do to ensure that the crucified men are dead?

What do you think the Jews are planning to do with the bodies? Where will Jesus end up if no one intervenes? How does this square with Isaiah 53?

ONE STEP FURTHER:

Word Studies:

If you have some extra time this week, see what you can find out about the Hebrew words that are translated "violence" and "deceit" in Isaiah 53:9 then record below what you discover.

violence

deceit

OBSERVE the TEXT of SCRIPTURE

Although Jesus would have been buried with the other crucified men, another man disrupts the scene.

READ Matthew 27:57-60. **MARK** every reference to *Joseph* (include synonyms and pronouns).

Matthew 27:57-60

57 *When it was evening, there came a rich man from Arimathea, named Joseph, who himself had also become a disciple of Jesus.*

58 *This man went to Pilate and asked for the body of Jesus. Then Pilate ordered it to be given to him.*

59 *And Joseph took the body and wrapped it in a clean linen cloth,*

60 *and laid it in his own new tomb, which he had hewn out in the rock; and he rolled a large stone against the entrance of the tomb and went away.*

DISCUSS with your GROUP or PONDER on your own . . .

Who asks for Jesus' body? Who does he have go through to get it?

How is this man connected to Jesus? What else do we know about him?

How does this compare with Isaiah 53:9?

The Servant clearly dies and is buried, but what does verse 9 say about Him with regard to "violence" (Hebrew: *hamas*) and "deceit" (Hebrew: *mirmah*)?

Are you ever tempted to sin because of external circumstances? If so, what kind of triggers do you usually fall for? How can considering Jesus' example help you when you are tempted to sin in response to others?

> ## ONE STEP FURTHER:
>
> **Sinless**
> Take some time this week to consider what the New Testament says about Jesus being sinless. I'll give you a couple of verses to start out with, but see how many others you can add to this string of pearls.
>
> **1 Corinthians 5:21**
>
> **Hebrews 4:15**

OBSERVE the TEXT of SCRIPTURE

Jesus was handed over to be crucified although He was known to be innocent. Let's look at a few cross-references from the Gospels from a cross-section of people.

READ the following verses and **MARK** references to *innocent* and *righteous*.

Matthew 27:3-4

3 Then when Judas, who had betrayed Him, saw that He had been condemned, he felt remorse and returned the thirty pieces of silver to the chief priests and elders,

4 saying, "I have sinned by betraying innocent blood." But they said, "What is that to us? See to that yourself!"

Matthew 27:17-19

17 So when the people gathered together, Pilate said to them, "Whom do you want me to release for you? Barabbas, or Jesus who is called Christ?"

18 For he knew that because of envy they had handed Him over.

19 While he was sitting on the judgment seat, his wife sent him a message, saying, "Have nothing to do with that righteous Man; for last night I suffered greatly in a dream because of Him."

ANOINTED
To Suffer · To Serve · To Save

Lesson Six: **No Violence, No Deceit**

Matthew 27:22-24

22 Pilate said to them, "Then what shall I do with Jesus who is called Christ?" They all said, "Crucify Him!"

23 And he said, "Why, what evil has He done?" But they kept shouting all the more, saying, "Crucify Him!"

24 When Pilate saw that he was accomplishing nothing, but rather that a riot was starting, he took water and washed his hands in front of the crowd, saying, "I am innocent of this Man's blood; see to that *yourselves.*"

DISCUSS with your GROUP or PONDER on your own . . .

According to Matthew 27:3-4, why does Judas have remorse over betraying Jesus?

In Matthew 27:17-19, what message does Pilate's wife send him with regard to Jesus? How does she describe Him?

How do these characterizations of Jesus compare with the Servant of Isaiah 53?

In Matthew 17:22-24, how do the people respond when Pilate asks what evil Jesus has done?

What does Pilate do before having Jesus scourged and handed over to the people? What does this indicate?

ANOINTED
To Suffer · To Serve · To Save

Digging Deeper

Without Sin

This week, consider Jesus' temptation in the wilderness, His agony in the garden, and His suffering on the cross. Jesus shows us His sinlessness firsthand.

In the Wilderness (Matthew 4)

In the Garden of Gethsemane (Matthew 26:36ff, Mark 14:32ff, Luke 22:40ff)

On the Cross (Matthew 27:33ff, Mark 15:22ff, Luke 23:33ff, John 19:17ff)

How did Jesus demonstrate His sinlessness in these situations?

ANOINTED
TO SUFFER · TO SERVE · TO SAVE

Lesson Six: **No Violence, No Deceit**

@THE END OF THE DAY . . .

As we finish up today, take some time to think back through all that we've studied this week in particular and in previous weeks. If you were in Jesus' sandals, what are some things He endured that would trigger a sin response in you? How did He handle situations and people differently than you do?

Now, think about current "sin triggers" in your life. Spend some time bringing them before the Father and asking Him to help you to walk by the power of His Spirit day by day and not in the empty resolve of your flesh.

FYI:

More Like Jesus

"Let your light shine before men in such a way that they may see your good works, and glorify your Father who is in heaven."

—Jesus, Matthew 5:16

LESSON SEVEN
The Final Sacrifice

". . . If He would render Himself as a guilt offering . . ."
–Isaiah 53:10

Every Jewish person raised under the Torah knew the sacrificial system. They learned about the sacrifices and offerings designed to cover their sins before a holy God. Many Christians today have a passing understanding of the sacrificial system and some have read enough of Leviticus to realize its complexity, but few grasp its intricacies and finer details. That's understandable, though, since we've never "lived" the system. Those who understand baseball best are those who have actually played the game! If you just watch it, it's harder to understand. If you only read about it, it's harder still.

There's no shame in finding Leviticus tough. That said, tough or not, Leviticus can help us unlock other parts of Scripture. So hold onto your hats; we're starting today in Isaiah but we're heading back to Leviticus. It's Lesson Seven and there is no turning back now!

Lesson Seven: **The Final Sacrifice**

REMEMBERING

Briefly outline Isaiah 53:1-9. You can use keywords, write it out word-for-word, or simply record your key takeaways from each verse or section.

How would you respond to someone who asked you what you're studying in the Bible these days?

WEEKLY OBSERVATION

Let's start again with Isaiah 53, but you knew that, didn't you?

OBSERVE the TEXT of SCRIPTURE

READ Isaiah 53 and **MARK** any time phrases you see and any references to *death* (include synonyms, allusions, and euphemisms). Then **UNDERLINE** any references that indicate that the Servant continues to live after His death.

Isaiah 53

1 Who has believed our message?
   And to whom has the arm of the LORD been revealed?

2 For He grew up before Him like a tender shoot,
   And like a root out of parched ground;
   He has no stately form or majesty
   That we should look upon Him,
   Nor appearance that we should be attracted to Him.

3   He was despised and forsaken of men,
    A man of sorrows and acquainted with grief;
    And like one from whom men hide their face
    He was despised, and we did not esteem Him.

4   Surely our griefs He Himself bore,
    And our sorrows He carried;
    Yet we ourselves esteemed Him stricken,
    Smitten of God, and afflicted.

5   But He was pierced through for our transgressions,
    He was crushed for our iniquities;
    The chastening for our well-being fell upon Him,
    And by His scourging we are healed.

6   All of us like sheep have gone astray,
    Each of us has turned to his own way;
    But the LORD has caused the iniquity of us all
    To fall on Him.

7   He was oppressed and He was afflicted,
    Yet He did not open His mouth;
    Like a lamb that is led to slaughter,
    And like a sheep that is silent before its shearers,
    So He did not open His mouth.

8   By oppression and judgment He was taken away;
    And as for His generation, who considered
    That He was cut off out of the land of the living
    For the transgression of my people, to whom the stroke was due?

9   His grave was assigned with wicked men,
    Yet He was with a rich man in His death,
    Because He had done no violence,
    Nor was there any deceit in His mouth.

10 But the LORD was pleased
    To crush Him, putting Him to grief;
    If He would render Himself as a guilt offering,
    He will see His offspring,
    He will prolong His days,
    And the good pleasure of the LORD will prosper in His hand.

11 As a result of the anguish of His soul,
    He will see it and be satisfied;
    By His knowledge the Righteous One,
    My Servant, will justify the many,
    As He will bear their iniquities.

12 Therefore, I will allot Him a portion with the great,
    And He will divide the booty with the strong;
    Because He poured out Himself to death,
    And was numbered with the transgressors;
    Yet He Himself bore the sin of many,
    And interceded for the transgressors.

ONE STEP FURTHER:

My Meditation All the Day!
How many benefits are there in meditating on God's Word? Psalm 119:97-104 gives compelling answers. If you have time this week, read this stanza—the Mem stanza of this 22-stanza acrostic poem—and record below how the Psalmist benefited from meditating on God's Word all the day!

ANOINTED
To Suffer · To Serve · To Save

81

DISCUSS with your GROUP or PONDER on your own . . .

Looking back at what you marked, list all of the possible references to the Servant's death. Some may be allusions, others definite. Put a star by those that definitely indicate that He died.

What phrases indicate that the Servant lives again after His physical death?

Before we move forward, think for a moment about how knowing the end of the story or a situation's outcome can change your view of current events. Hold that thought as we continue on!

LOOKING CLOSER . . .

Although the Servant's death appears tragic on the surface, God's purpose far exceeds man's wildest imagination.

OBSERVE the TEXT of SCRIPTURE

READ Isaiah 53:10 and **MARK** references to *the Servant* (they will all be pronouns— *Him, He*, etc.) and **UNDERLINE** everything that the Servant does or will do. Also **MARK** references to the *LORD*.

Isaiah 53:10

10 *But the LORD was pleased*
      To crush Him, putting Him to grief;
      If He would render Himself as a guilt offering,
      He will see His offspring,
      He will prolong His days,
      And the good pleasure of the LORD will prosper in His hand.

Digging Deeper

Memorization

Here's my basic breakdown on Isaiah 53:10. The boldface words help me lock in on the key content. See if it helps and then write yours below.

What the Lord wills

10 But the LORD was **pleased**

What the Lord does

To crush   Him,

putting Him   **to grief;**

Conditional "IF" statement that has been met

If He would render Himself as a **guilt offering,**

THEN

(1) He will **see** His **offspring,**
(2) He will **prolong** His **days,**
And
(3) the **good pleasure** of the LORD **will prosper** in His hand.

FYI:

A Look at Other Translations—Isaiah 53:10a
The boldface is mine to show the variations in the translation of the Hebrew word **hapes**.

"But the LORD was **pleased** to crush Him . . ."
   —New American Standard (NASB)

"Yet it was the **will** of the LORD to crush him . . ."
   —English Standard Version (ESV)

"Yet it was the LORD's **will** to crush him . . ."
   —New International Version (NLT)

"But it was the LORD's **good plan** to crush him . . ."
   —New Living Translation (NLT)

"Though the LORD **desired** to crush him . . ."
   —NET Bible® (NET)

"But the LORD **chose** to crush him . . ."
   —Jewish Publication Society (JPS)

ANOINTED
To Suffer · To Serve · To Save

83

Lesson Seven: **The Final Sacrifice**

DISCUSS with your GROUP or PONDER on your own . . .

Compare the beginning and end of verse 10 (line one and line 6) with regard to the LORD and His interaction with the Servant. What do you notice?

What will the Servant do? What outcome will result? For the LORD? For the Servant? For mankind?

LOOKING CLOSER . . .

Why is the LORD "pleased" to crush the Servant? If this bothers you, you're not alone. It's a question that honest study addresses. Let's look at more of the story to see if we can discover why our gracious and compassionate God characterized by lovingkindness is "pleased" to crush His Servant.

OBSERVE the TEXT of SCRIPTURE

READ Isaiah 1:1-20 and **MARK** *sacrifices* and *offerings*. Also **MARK** references to *My people* (and synonyms) distinctively.

Isaiah 1:1-20

1 *The vision of Isaiah the son of Amoz concerning Judah and Jerusalem, which he saw during the reigns of Uzziah, Jotham, Ahaz and Hezekiah, kings of Judah.*

2 *Listen, O heavens, and hear, O earth; For the LORD speaks, "Sons I have reared and brought up, But they have revolted against Me.*

3 *"An ox knows its owner, And a donkey its master's manger, But Israel does not know, My people do not understand."*

4 *Alas, sinful nation, People weighed down with iniquity, Offspring of evildoers, Sons who act corruptly! They have abandoned the LORD, They have despised the Holy One of Israel, They have turned away from Him.*

5 *Where will you be stricken again, As you continue in your rebellion? The whole head is sick And the whole heart is faint.*

6 *From the sole of the foot even to the head There is nothing sound in it, Only bruises, welts and raw wounds, Not pressed out or bandaged, Nor softened with oil.*

ANOINTED
To Suffer · To Serve · To Save

7   *Your land is desolate, Your cities are burned with fire, Your fields—strangers are devouring them in your presence; It is desolation, as overthrown by strangers.*

8   *The daughter of Zion is left like a shelter in a vineyard, Like a watchman's hut in a cucumber field, like a besieged city.*

9   *Unless the LORD of hosts Had left us a few survivors, We would be like Sodom, We would be like Gomorrah.*

10 *Hear the word of the LORD, You rulers of Sodom; Give ear to the instruction of our God, You people of Gomorrah.*

11 *"What are your multiplied sacrifices to Me?" Says the LORD. "I have had enough of burnt offerings of rams And the fat of fed cattle; And I take no pleasure in the blood of bulls, lambs or goats.*

12 *"When you come to appear before Me, Who requires of you this trampling of My courts?*

13 *"Bring your worthless offerings no longer, Incense is an abomination to Me. New moon and sabbath, the calling of assemblies— I cannot endure iniquity and the solemn assembly.*

14 *"I hate your new moon festivals and your appointed feasts, They have become a burden to Me; I am weary of bearing them.*

15 *"So when you spread out your hands in prayer, I will hide My eyes from you; Yes, even though you multiply prayers, I will not listen. Your hands are covered with blood.*

16 *"Wash yourselves, make yourselves clean; Remove the evil of your deeds from My sight. Cease to do evil,*

17 *Learn to do good; Seek justice, Reprove the ruthless, Defend the orphan, Plead for the widow.*

18 *"Come now, and let us reason together," Says the LORD, "Though your sins are as scarlet, They will be as white as snow; Though they are red like crimson, They will be like wool.*

19 *"If you consent and obey, You will eat the best of the land;*

20 *"But if you refuse and rebel, You will be devoured by the sword." Truly, the mouth of the LORD has spoken.*

DISCUSS with your GROUP or PONDER on your own . . .

Who is the message directed to? Describe their situation.

INDUCTIVE FOCUS:

Unclear in Light of the Clear

A key principle in inductive Bible study is that we always interpret unclear passages in light of clear ones and not the other way around. One of the clearest truths we know about God comes from His own self-description found in Exodus 34:6-7 as He reveals Himself to Moses.

"*Then the LORD passed by in front of him and proclaimed, "The LORD, the LORD God, compassionate and gracious, slow to anger, and abounding in lovingkindness and truth; who keeps lovingkindness for thousands, who forgives iniquity, transgression and sin; yet He will by no means leave the guilty unpunished, visiting the iniquity of fathers on the children and on the grandchildren to the third and fourth generations."*

What basic truths about God are clear from these verses? How do you think they may shed light on Isaiah 53?

FYI:

Crushed

Don't forget how the word "crushed" (Hebrew: *daka*) has already been used in Isaiah 53. Verse 10 says that "the LORD was pleased to crush Him," but verse 5 has already told us the reason the Servant was crushed: "He was crushed for our iniquities."

Lesson Seven: **The Final Sacrifice**

How does God describe the people?

What does He say about their worship?

According to Isaiah 1:11, what does God not take pleasure in? Why?

What situation does that leave the people in? What do they need?

What do people who offend God today need? Explain your answer from Scripture.

OBSERVE the TEXT of SCRIPTURE

Now let's look at a passage from the New Testament that will help us understand what purpose the Law and the sacrificial system had in the first place.

READ Hebrews 10:1-14 and **MARK** every occurrence of *sacrifices.*

Hebrews 9:27–10:1-14

27   *And inasmuch as it is appointed for men to die once and after this comes judgment,*

28   *so Christ also, having been offered once to bear the sins of many, will appear a second time for salvation without reference to sin, to those who eagerly await Him.*

Digging Deeper

Take a Tour Through Hebrews

If studying only one chapter has you itching to read more of God's Word, take some time this week to read the epistle to the Hebrews to discover how Jesus is "better than," well, everything! We've already seen that He is a better sacrifice. As you read, record how Jesus exceeds angels, Moses, and all the rest!

FYI:

Bonus Info!

If you've never read the book of Leviticus and kind of dread doing it, this advice is for you. Read Leviticus alongside of Hebrews so you can see the New Covenant truths that the Old Covenant points to—first the shadows (Leviticus), then the reality (Hebrews)! I think you'll be amazed at how much you're going to love them both—especially together!

1   *For the Law, since it has* only *a shadow of the good things to come* and *not the very form of things, can never, by the same sacrifices which they offer continually year by year, make perfect those who draw near.*

2   *Otherwise, would they not have ceased to be offered, because the worshipers, having once been cleansed, would no longer have had consciousness of sins?*

3   *But in those* sacrifices *there is a reminder of sins year by year.*

4   *For it is impossible for the blood of bulls and goats to take away sins.*

5   *Therefore, when He comes into the world, He says, "SACRIFICE AND OFFERING YOU HAVE NOT DESIRED, BUT A BODY YOU HAVE PREPARED FOR ME;*

6   *IN WHOLE BURNT OFFERINGS AND* sacrifices *FOR SIN YOU HAVE TAKEN NO PLEASURE.*

7   *"THEN I SAID, 'BEHOLD, I HAVE COME (IN THE SCROLL OF THE BOOK IT IS WRITTEN OF ME) TO DO YOUR WILL, O GOD.' "*

ANOINTED
TO SUFFER · TO SERVE · TO SAVE

NOTES

ONE STEP FURTHER:

Revelation 13:7-8

Take some time this week to look up Revelation 13:7-8. Full disclosure: you'll probably want to back up a few verses to pick up the context. Once you've read the section and focused on verses 7 and 8, consider how long God's plan has been in place. Record below what verse 8 says about how long the book of life has been around and what it says about the Lamb.

8 After saying above, "SACRIFICES AND OFFERINGS AND WHOLE BURNT OFFERINGS AND sacrifices FOR SIN YOU HAVE NOT DESIRED, NOR HAVE YOU TAKEN PLEASURE in them" (which are offered according to the Law),

9 then He said, "BEHOLD, I HAVE COME TO DO YOUR WILL." He takes away the first in order to establish the second.

10 By this will we have been sanctified through the offering of the body of Jesus Christ once for all.

11 Every priest stands daily ministering and offering time after time the same sacrifices, which can never take away sins;

12 but He, having offered one sacrifice for sins for all time, SAT DOWN AT THE RIGHT HAND OF GOD,

13 waiting from that time onward UNTIL HIS ENEMIES BE MADE A FOOTSTOOL FOR HIS FEET.

14 For by one offering He has perfected for all time those who are sanctified.

DISCUSS with your GROUP or PONDER on your own . . .

What does Hebrews 10 teach about sacrifices and their effectiveness?

How does Hebrews 10:1 describe the Law? Can the Law make a person perfect? Why/why not?.

If a sacrifice truly cleanses a person, what results do you expect?

What limitations do sacrifices offered under the law have? What can't the Law and its sacrificial system do?

Conversely, what uncomfortable effect does it have?

How does Christ's sacrifice differ? How does it affect those who are sanctified? If you are in relationship with God through Jesus, what effect does this have on you day by day? Moment by moment?

LOOKING CLOSER . . .

The book of Leviticus explains a variety of different offerings—the burnt offering, grain (or meal) and drink offering, the peace offering (which includes the wave and heave offering), the sin (or purification) offering, and the guilt (or trespass / reparation) offering. Before we call it a day, let's look more closely at Isaiah 53:10's Servant who renders Himself as a guilt offering. Yes, we're going back to Leviticus!

OBSERVE the TEXT of SCRIPTURE

READ Leviticus 5:1-5, 14-19 and 6:1-7 and **MARK** every occurrence of *guilt*, *guilty*, and *guilt offering*.

Leviticus 5:1-5, 14-19

1 *'Now if a person sins after he hears a public adjuration* to testify *when he is a witness, whether he has seen or* otherwise *known, if he does not tell it, then he will bear his guilt.*

2 *'Or if a person touches any unclean thing, whether a carcass of an unclean beast or the carcass of unclean cattle or a carcass of unclean swarming things, though it is hidden from him and he is unclean, then he will be guilty.*

3 *'Or if he touches human uncleanness, of whatever* sort *his uncleanness* may *be with which he becomes unclean, and it is hidden from him, and then he comes to know it, he will be guilty.*

4 *'Or if a person swears thoughtlessly with his lips to do evil or to do good, in whatever matter a man may speak thoughtlessly with an oath, and it is hidden from him, and then he comes to know* it, *he will be guilty in one of these.*

5 *'So it shall be when he becomes guilty in one of these, that he shall confess that in which he has sinned.*

Verses 6 through 13 provide the specifics of what guilt offerings are and how they should be presented along with other offerings.

14 Then the LORD spoke to Moses, saying,

15 "If a person acts unfaithfully and sins unintentionally against the LORD'S holy things, then he shall bring his guilt offering to the LORD: a ram without defect from the flock, according to your valuation in silver by shekels, in terms of *the shekel of the sanctuary, for a guilt offering.*

16 "He shall make restitution for that which he has sinned against the holy thing, and shall add to it a fifth part of it and give it to the priest. The priest shall then make atonement for him with the ram of the guilt offering, and it will be forgiven him.

17 "Now if a person sins and does any of the things which the LORD has commanded not to be done, though he was unaware, still he is guilty and shall bear his punishment.

18 "He is then to bring to the priest a ram without defect from the flock, according to your valuation, for a guilt offering. So the priest shall make atonement for him concerning his error in which he sinned unintentionally and did not know it, and it will be forgiven him.

19 "It is a guilt offering; he was certainly guilty before the LORD."

Leviticus 6:1-7

1 Then the LORD spoke to Moses, saying,

2 "When a person sins and acts unfaithfully against the LORD, and deceives his companion in regard to a deposit or a security entrusted to him, or through robbery, or if he has extorted from his companion,

3 or has found what was lost and lied about it and sworn falsely, so that he sins in regard to any one of the things a man may do;

4 then it shall be, when he sins and becomes guilty, that he shall restore what he took by robbery or what he got by extortion, or the deposit which was entrusted to him or the lost thing which he found,

5 or anything about which he swore falsely; he shall make restitution for it in full and add to it one-fifth more. He shall give it to the one to whom it belongs on the day he presents his guilt offering.

6 "Then he shall bring to the priest his guilt offering to the LORD, a ram without defect from the flock, according to your valuation, for a guilt offering,

7 and the priest shall make atonement for him before the LORD, and he will be forgiven for any one of the things which he may have done to incur guilt."

ONE STEP FURTHER:

Ephesians 1:2-12

You won't regret taking a little more time to carefully read the first 12 verses of Ephesians. As you read, note what God's plan is and how long it has been in place. Also note what the outcome will be—for the Father, for Christ, and for us.

DISCUSS with your GROUP or PONDER on your own . . .

Under what circumstances did a person need a guilt offering? Based on the first phrase of verse 2, were any humans entirely exempt? Why/why not?

Based on the text, is it possible to be guilty without knowing it? Do you know people today who are guilty before God but have no idea of their condition?

When was the guilt offering to be brought to the LORD?

What did the offeror of the guilt offering do in addition to bringing a sacrifice to God? (See 5:5, 5:16, and 6:5.)

What is the result for the person who brings a guilt offering to the LORD according to Leviticus 5:16?

How does the guilt offering help us understand what the Servant's death accomplished?

Lesson Seven: **The Final Sacrifice**

@THE END OF THE DAY . . .

Take some time to worship your God who loved you enough to provide a Perfect Lamb to take away not only your sin but also the sin of the world!

*The next day [John the Baptist] saw Jesus
coming to him and said, "Behold, the Lamb of God
who takes away the sin of the world!"*
–John 1:29

LESSON EIGHT
Forgiven!

". . . He Himself bore the sin of many,
And interceded for the transgressors."
–Isaiah 53:12c

What seemed like the end of the story was just the beginning! Death could not hold the humbled Servant of the LORD who gave Himself as a guilt offering! The final verses of Isaiah 53 declare God's purposes fulfilled, the Servant honored, and the many forgiven! Because of the Servant, we can be forgiven. Because of the Servant's suffering, we can be made whole!

Lesson Eight: **Forgiven!**

REMEMBERING

Take a few moments to review Isaiah 53. If you can write it from memory, great! If you can fill in the main thoughts from memory, that's great, too! If you'd rather think through your biggest takeaways from each verse with the text in front of you, go for it!

Isaiah 53:1

Isaiah 53:2

Isaiah 53:3

Isaiah 53:4

Isaiah 53:5

Isaiah 53:6

Isaiah 53:7

Isaiah 53:8

Isaiah 53:9

Isaiah 53:10

WEEKLY OBSERVATION

Let's once again read through Isaiah 53.

OBSERVE the TEXT of SCRIPTURE

READ Isaiah 53. Take the tools that you've been learning and **MARK** whatever you think is most significant. You can **MARK** everything we've **MARKED** together (to have a compilation) or simply **MARK** the words and/or phrases you found to be most helpful or most significant as we've been studying together.

Isaiah 53

1   *Who has believed our message?*
    And to whom has the arm of the LORD been revealed?

2   *For He grew up before Him like a tender shoot,*
    And like a root out of parched ground;
    He has no stately form or majesty
    That we should look upon Him,
    Nor appearance that we should be attracted to Him.

3   *He was despised and forsaken of men,*
    A man of sorrows and acquainted with grief;
    And like one from whom men hide their face
    He was despised, and we did not esteem Him.

4   *Surely our griefs He Himself bore,*
    And our sorrows He carried;
    Yet we ourselves esteemed Him stricken,
    Smitten of God, and afflicted.

5   *But He was pierced through for our transgressions,*
    He was crushed for our iniquities;
    The chastening for our well-being fell upon Him,
    And by His scourging we are healed.

6   *All of us like sheep have gone astray,*
    Each of us has turned to his own way;
    But the LORD has caused the iniquity of us all
    To fall on Him.

7   *He was oppressed and He was afflicted,*
    Yet He did not open His mouth;
    Like a lamb that is led to slaughter,
    And like a sheep that is silent before its shearers,
    So He did not open His mouth.

8   *By oppression and judgment He was taken away;*
    And as for His generation, who considered
    That He was cut off out of the land of the living
    For the transgression of my people, to whom the stroke was due?

9   *His grave was assigned with wicked men,*
    Yet He was with a rich man in His death,
    Because He had done no violence,
    Nor was there any deceit in His mouth.

ANOINTED
To Suffer · To Serve · To Save

ONE STEP FURTHER:

Word Study: "Satisfied"
Take time this week to find the Hebrew word translated "satisfied" in Isaiah 53:11. See how it is used in the rest of Isaiah and elsewhere in the Old Testament. Record what you learned below.

10 But the LORD was pleased
    To crush Him, putting Him *to* grief;
    If He would render Himself *as* a guilt offering,
    He will see His offspring,
    He will prolong His days,
    And the good pleasure of the LORD will prosper in His hand.

11 As a result of the anguish of His soul,
    He will see *it and* be satisfied;
    By His knowledge the Righteous One,
    My Servant, will justify the many,
    As He will bear their iniquities.

12 Therefore, I will allot Him a portion with the great,
    And He will divide the booty with the strong;
    Because He poured out Himself to death,
    And was numbered with the transgressors;
    Yet He Himself bore the sin of many,
    And interceded for the transgressors.

DISCUSS with your GROUP or PONDER on your own . . .

What did you choose to mark and why?

What questions do you still have about the passage?

What, if any, questions do you still have about the inductive tool of marking the text?

FYI:

Crucified with Christ
"I have been crucified with Christ; and it is no longer I who live, but Christ lives in me; and the life which I now live in the flesh I live by faith in the Son of God, who loved me and gave Himself up for me."

—Galatians 2:20

LOOKING CLOSER ...

Although the big picture that verses 11 and 12 paint is clear enough, there are some questions that the text brings up but doesn't answer. So if you've been scratching your head a bit on the details of these verses, you're not alone! Some of the brightest minds in biblical studies do, too! We'll focus today on the main point, while also addressing a few of the head scratchers along the way.

OBSERVE the TEXT of SCRIPTURE

READ Isaiah 53:11 and **MARK** all of the pronouns.

Isaiah 53:11

11   *As a result of the anguish of His soul,*
     He will see it and be satisfied;
     By His knowledge the Righteous One,
     My Servant, will justify the many,
     As He will bear their iniquities.

DISCUSS with your GROUP or PONDER on your own ...

Now let's wrestle with the pronouns to see who they refer to. Who is speaking in verses 11? How do you know? Why do you think there is a shift?

Who is the "He" in verse 11, line 2? How do you know? What will His disposition be? What has He been through?

Read the FYI to the right, then: do you think the nouns and pronouns in verse 11 are clearly identified?

Who is the Righteous One and how will He justify the many?

FYI:

A Brief Grammar Lesson

For some of us, technical speech about grammar is a few years removed from our everyday lives. We know grammar, we use grammar every day when we speak, listen, read, and write, but to define it can be elusive. I was a card-carrying grammar nerd (seriously, I was a member of Quill and Scroll—a high school journalism honor society), but even I didn't lock down my understanding of grammar definitions until I took Greek in college. Even with that there are terms that I still have to "Google." Really, who can consistently remember what a gerund is?!

One of the most common grammar pairs that you need to be aware of in Bible study (or any literary interpretation for that matter) is the pronoun/antecedent couple.

Let's define.

A **pronoun** is simply a word that takes the place of a noun or a noun phrase. Here are some examples:

I, you, he, she, it, we, them

Instead of repeating nouns over and over in our speech and writing, we substitute pronouns. It's all very clear . . . until it isn't.

Pronouns can become unclear when we're not sure what noun they are referring back to. That's where the fancy word antecedent comes in. The **antecedent** is the original noun the pronoun is filling in for. It lets you know who the "I," "he," or "she" is!

Whenever you find yourself asking, "Hey, is that 'He' God the Father or Jesus?" you've run into a case of an unclear antecedent.

ANOINTED
To Suffer · To Serve · To Save

LOOKING CLOSER . . .

While there are some tough interpretive questions in the text, none muddles the key theological truth that the Righteous One bore sins that were not His own and that He will justify the many. Let's look at this more deeply by exploring Romans 5.

OBSERVE the TEXT of SCRIPTURE

As we pick up in Romans 5, Paul is explaining the gospel for his readers who are likely a mixture of both Jewish and Gentile believers. He has already laid down the foundation that the whole world is under sin (Romans 1–3:20) and is now concluding a section where He has been explaining salvation by faith in Jesus (Romans 3:21–5:5).

READ Romans 5:6-21 and **MARK** the phrase *the many*. Also **MARK** the word *righteous/righteousness* and *justified* the same way as each other.

Romans 5:6-21

6   *For while we were still helpless, at the right time Christ died for the ungodly.*

7   *For one will hardly die for a righteous man; though perhaps for the good man someone would dare even to die.*

8   *But God demonstrates His own love toward us, in that while we were yet sinners, Christ died for us.*

9   *Much more then, having now been justified by His blood, we shall be saved from the wrath of God through Him.*

10   *For if while we were enemies we were reconciled to God through the death of His Son, much more, having been reconciled, we shall be saved by His life.*

11   *And not only this, but we also exult in God through our Lord Jesus Christ, through whom we have now received the reconciliation.*

12   *Therefore, just as through one man sin entered into the world, and death through sin, and so death spread to all men, because all sinned—*

13   *for until the Law sin was in the world, but sin is not imputed when there is no law.*

14   *Nevertheless death reigned from Adam until Moses, even over those who had not sinned in the likeness of the offense of Adam, who is a type of Him who was to come.*

15   *But the free gift is not like the transgression. For if by the transgression of the one the many died, much more did the grace of God and the gift by the grace of the one Man, Jesus Christ, abound to the many.*

16   *The gift is not like that which came through the one who sinned; for on the one hand the judgment arose from one transgression resulting in condemnation, but on the other hand the free gift arose from many transgressions resulting in justification.*

17   *For if by the transgression of the one, death reigned through the one, much more those who receive the abundance of grace and of the gift of righteousness will reign in life through the One, Jesus Christ.*

INDUCTIVE FOCUS:

Unclear in Light of the Clear—Another Thought

When studying inductively, we always want to interpret unclear portions of Scripture in light of texts that are clear. We also need to realize there are times when details of a text may be unclear while its main message is easily understood. Let's look at Isaiah 53:11-12 for some examples. In these verses we have several textual issues that are not clear because the words involved can be translated from the Hebrew differently. Isolated unclear phrases, though, don't *necessarily* obfuscate the passage as a whole. Let me see if I can explain.

• *What will the Servant see and be satisfied with?*

The text doesn't tell us clearly. Commentators offer options and opinions, but no one knows for sure. How does it change our application of these verses? It doesn't. The Servant has borne our iniquities and is satisfied—we can rest in that fact—regardless of what the object of His satisfaction is.

• *In the middle of verse 11, are the many justified by "knowledge of the Righteous One" or is it "by the Righteous One's knowledge" that He will justify the many?*

"Wait!" you say, "aren't both of those true?" Yes, I think you see both of these concepts elsewhere in Scripture. Thus, which is intended here is less of an issue because neither veers from the clear teaching of the full counsel of God's Word.

There are more, but let's leave it at these two examples for now. Deal?

18 *So then as through one transgression there resulted condemnation to all men, even so through one act of righteousness there resulted justification of life to all men.*

19 *For as through the one man's disobedience the many were made sinners, even so through the obedience of the One the many will be made righteous.*

20 *The Law came in so that the transgression would increase; but where sin increased, grace abounded all the more,*

21 *so that, as sin reigned in death, even so grace would reign through righteousness to eternal life through Jesus Christ our Lord.*

DISCUSS with your GROUP or PONDER on your own . . .

According to verses 6-10, who did Christ die for and how are they described?

What does this demonstrate about God? Based on this past action, what can the justified expect in the future?

According to verse 9, what did Christ's blood do?

How does verse 10 describe what Christ's death accomplished? What about His life?

Why do humans need a Savior? How did we end up so corrupted?

ONE STEP FURTHER:

Just/Righteous

Take some time to look at the words "justification" and "righteousness" in Romans 5 to see how they're related. Then record below what you discover. This will be quick and well worth your time!

ANOINTED
To Suffer · To Serve · To Save

99

Lesson Eight: **Forgiven!**

Do you think most people are aware on some level of their need for a Savior? Why/why not? Think through what the Bible specifically teaches as you answer—Romans 1:18ff is a great place to start!

How did you become aware? How could this help you counsel others?

What two-fold result did Adam's sin bring?

What, by contrast, did the free gift bring and result in?

Thinking back to Isaiah, how does the Righteous One make the many righteous?

Are you living in the truth that because of Jesus, God can justly declare you righteous? How does your life reflect this miracle of forgiveness and grace?

LOOKING EVEN CLOSER . . .

Let's take a look at the final verse of Isaiah 53.

OBSERVE the TEXT of SCRIPTURE

READ Isaiah 53:12 and **MARK** all of the pronouns (*I, My, He, His, it, their,* etc.)

Isaiah 53:12

12 *Therefore, I will allot Him a portion with the great,*
And He will divide the booty with the strong;
Because He poured out Himself to death,
And was numbered with the transgressors;
Yet He Himself bore the sin of many,
And interceded for the transgressors.

DISCUSS with your GROUP or PONDER on your own . . .

Again, who is speaking in this verse? What is He going to do for the Servant?

How does verse 12 describe the Servant's work? How does this compare with what we've seen about the life of Jesus?

What what will happen to the Servant after His work is complete?

Why will He receive these things?

FYI:

A Look at Other Translations—Isaiah 53:12 (Dave will size this to fit)

If you've read Isaiah 53:12 in more than one translation, you may have been surprised at the differences. We wonder which is right: does the Servant divide the spoil with the strong or are the strong the spoil that the Servant receives? Scholars disagree as the translations (below) show. What's a person to do when prayerful, inductive study doesn't lead to a definitive answer? We focus on what is clear. In this passage, what is most important is also *most clear:* the Servant died, the Servant bore others' sins, the Servant intercedes for them.

"Therefore I will give Him the many as a portion, and He will receive the mighty as spoil, because He submitted Himself to death, and was counted among the rebels; yet He bore the sin of many and interceded for the rebels."

   —Holman Christian Standard Bible

"Therefore I will divide him a portion with the many, and he shall divide the spoil with the strong, because he poured out his soul to death and was numbered with the transgressors; yet he bore the sin of many, and makes intercession for the transgressors."

   —English Standard Version

"Assuredly, I will give him the many as his portion, He shall receive the multitude as his spoil. For he exposed himself to death And was numbered among the sinners, Whereas he bore the guilt of the many And made intercession for sinners."

   —Jewish Publication Society

ANOINTED
TO SUFFER · TO SERVE · TO SAVE

Digging Deeper

Memorization

Take some time to break down Isaiah 53:11-12 so the verses are easy for you to recall as you're memorizing. I'll space it out to give you a little more working room.

11 *As a result of the anguish of His soul,*

He will see it and be satisfied;

By His knowledge the Righteous One,

My Servant, will justify the many,

As He will bear their iniquities.

12 *Therefore, I will allot Him a portion with the great,*

And He will divide the booty with the strong;

Because He poured out Himself to death,

And was numbered with the transgressors;

Yet He Himself bore the sin of many,

And interceded for the transgressors.

Although the Servant suffered at the hands of man and verse 10 tells us that "the LORD was pleased to crush Him," how does verse 12 characterize His death?

LOOKING EVEN CLOSER . . .

As we bring this study to an end, let's look at one final passage from Paul's second letter to the Corinthians.

OBSERVE the TEXT of SCRIPTURE

READ 2 Corinthians 5:14-21 and **MARK** every occurrence of *Christ* including pronouns.

2 Corinthians 5:14-21

14 *For the love of Christ controls us, having concluded this, that one died for all, therefore all died;*

15 *and He died for all, so that they who live might no longer live for themselves, but for Him who died and rose again on their behalf.*

16 *Therefore from now on we recognize no one according to the flesh; even though we have known Christ according to the flesh, yet now we know Him in this way no longer.*

17 *Therefore if anyone is in Christ, he is a new creature; the old things passed away; behold, new things have come.*

18 *Now all these things are from God, who reconciled us to Himself through Christ and gave us the ministry of reconciliation,*

19 *namely, that God was in Christ reconciling the world to Himself, not counting their trespasses against them, and He has committed to us the word of reconciliation.*

20 *Therefore, we are ambassadors for Christ, as though God were making an appeal through us; we beg you on behalf of Christ, be reconciled to God.*

21 *He made Him who knew no sin to be sin on our behalf, so that we might become the righteousness of God in Him.*

DISCUSS with your GROUP or PONDER on your own . . .

If you have been reconciled to God in Christ, what are some ways your life has changed?

How does verse 17 describe this change?

If the love of Christ is controlling you, how is that changing your behavior day to day?

How does this passage describe reconciliation? Which party does the reconciling? How does this differ from typical human reconciliation?

What ministry has God given to the reconciled? How can you obey in this area? How are you obeying?

Finally, how does 2 Corinthians 5:21 summarize what the prophet Isaiah wrote about hundreds of years prior? How can you live more fully in the reality of this truth every single day?

@THE END OF THE DAY . . .

Review what you've learned sometime next week. Right now, worship Jesus . . .

Being found in appearance as a man,
He humbled Himself by becoming obedient to the point of death, even
death on a cross.
For this reason also, God highly exalted Him, and bestowed
on Him the name which is above every name, so that

at the name of Jesus EVERY KNEE WILL BOW,

of those who are in heaven and on earth and
under the earth, and that

every tongue will confess that Jesus Christ is Lord,

to the glory of God the Father.

−Philippians 2:8-11

ANOINTED
To Suffer · To Serve · To Save

105

RESOURCES

Helpful Study Tools

How to Study Your Bible
Eugene, Oregon: Harvest House
Publishers

The New Inductive Study Bible
Eugene, Oregon: Harvest House
Publishers

Logos Bible Software
Available at www.logos.com.

Greek Word Study Tools

Kittel, G., Friedrich, G., & Bromiley,
G.W.
*Theological Dictionary of the New
Testament, Abridged* (also known as
Little Kittel)
Grand Rapids, Michigan: W.B.
Eerdmans Publishing Company

Hebrew Word Study Tools

Harris, R.L., Archer, G.L., & Walker,
B.K.
*Theological Wordbook of the Old
Testament* (also known as TWOT)
Chicago, Illinois: Moody Press

General Word Study Tools

Strong, James
*The New Strong's Exhaustive
Concordance of the Bible*
Nashville, Tennessee: Thomas Nelson

Recommended Commentary Sets

Expositor's Bible Commentary
Grand Rapids, Michigan: Zondervan

NIV Application Commentary
Grand Rapids, Michigan: Zondervan

The New American Commentary
Nashville, Tennessee: Broadman and
Holman Publishers

One-Volume Commentary

Carson, D.A., France, R.T., Motyer,
J.A., & Wenham, G.J. Ed.
*New Bible Commentary: 21st Century
Edition*
Downers Grove, Illinois: Inter-Varsity
Press

Rydelnik, M.,,Vanlaningham, M., Ed.
The Moody Bible Commentary
Chicago, Illinois: Moody Publishers

HOW TO DO AN ONLINE WORD STUDY

For use with www.blueletterbible.org

1. Type in Bible verse. Change the version to NASB. Click the "Search" button.

2. When you arrive at the next screen, you will see a "Tools" button to the left of your verse .

3. Hover over the "Tools" button and select the "Interlinear" option to take you to the concordance link.

3. Click on the Strong's number which is the link to the original word in Greek or Hebrew.

Clicking this number will bring up another screen that will give you a brief definition of the word as well as list every occurrence of the Greek word in the New Testament or Hebrew word in the Old Testament. Before running to the dictionary definition, scan places where this word is used in Scripture and examine the general contexts where it is used.

ABOUT PRECEPT

Precept Ministries International was raised up by God for the sole purpose of establishing people in God's Word to produce reverence for Him. It serves as an arm of the church without respect to denomination. God has enabled Precept to reach across denominational lines without compromising the truths of His inerrant Word. We believe every word of the Bible was inspired and given to man as all that is necessary for him to become mature and thoroughly equipped for every good work of life. This ministry does not seek to impose its doctrines on others, but rather to direct people to the Master Himself, who leads and guides by His Spirit into all truth through a systematic study of His Word. The ministry produces a variety of Bible studies and holds conferences and intensive Training Workshops designed to establish attendees in the Word through Inductive Bible Study.

Jack Arthur and his wife, Kay, founded Precept Ministries in 1970. Kay and the ministry staff of writers produce **Precept Upon Precept** studies, **In & Out** studies, **Lord** series studies, the **New Inductive Study Series** studies, **40-Minute** studies, and **Discover 4 Yourself Inductive Bible Studies for Kids**. From years of diligent study and teaching experience, Kay and the staff have developed these unique, inductive courses that are now used in nearly 185 countries and 70 languages.

 PRECEPT.ORG

PAM GILLASPIE

Pam Gillaspie, a passionate Bible student and teacher, authors Precept's *Sweeter Than Chocolate!*® and *Cookies on the Lower Shelf*™ Bible study series. Pam holds a BA in Biblical Studies from Wheaton College in Wheaton, Illinois. She and her husband live in suburban Chicago, Illinois with their daughter and Great Dane. They also have a married son and a daughter-in-love. Pam's greatest joy is encouraging others to read God's Word widely and study it deeply . . . precept upon precept.

For speaking inquiries, questions, or just to connect, you can find Pam online at:

www.pamgillaspie.com

 pamgillaspie

 pamgillaspie